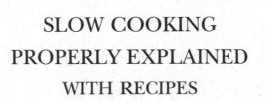

SLOW COOKING
PROPERLY EXPLAINED
WITH RECIPES

SLOW COOKING PROPERLY EXPLAINED

WITH RECIPES

Dianne Page

RIGHT WAY

Constable & Robinson Ltd
3 The Lanchesters
162 Fulham Palace Road
London W6 9ER
www.right-way.co.uk
www.constablerobinson.com

First published in the UK 1979
Fully revised 2003

This edition published by Right Way,
an imprint of Constable & Robinson, 2008

A copy of the British Library Cataloguing in Publication Data
is available from the British Library

ISBN: 978-0-7160-2047-9

Printed and bound in the EU

CONTENTS

DEDICATION

My thanks to family and friends who participated with such enthusiasm in the many tasting sessions during the writing of the book.

1

INTRODUCTION

Slow cookers are experiencing a revival. And it's not surprising. After witnessing years of fast food and lifestyles that are hectic beyond belief, this renewed interest in slow cooking is an understandable reaction. We yearn for the straightforwardness of our grandmother's (or indeed our great grandmother's) day, when slow cooking was a way of life and those who cooked knew how to make delicious meals out of very little. The food would be prepared in the morning and left to cook gently all day in the range beside the kitchen fire. By the time the family returned home in the evening, a delicious meal would be ready and waiting. Today, few of us have a cooking range but we can all be proud owners of a slow cooker and the advantages of this time-honoured method can still be appreciated.

So what is a slow cooker? Not somebody who cooks food slowly but an electrical appliance that is designed to cook gently and safely, unattended, for many hours without burning, boiling away or drying up. Most slow cookers have at least two settings so you can cook on HIGH for a few hours or in time for lunch, or on LOW for several hours, all day or overnight.

What is it good at? Well, a slow cooker not only makes delicious soups, stews and casseroles. It's also good at cooking fish and delicate fruit and vegetables, all of which stay nice and whole, even after long cooking. Joints of meat and whole chicken can be 'roasted' in a slow cooker with maximum retention of juices and minimum shrinkage. And by using the slow cooker as a water bath, you can prepare delicious pâté and the lightest of sponges and puddings. Even mulled wine and hot punches can be made in (and served straight from) a slow cooker to make any party go with a swing.

Why Cook Slowly?
Food that has been cooked slowly tastes wonderfully mellow because the flavours have had time to blend and develop. A

meat casserole that is cooked gently over a long period in moist heat becomes meltingly tender. In fact, slow cooking will tenderise even the toughest cuts of meat – shin of beef, oxtail and neck of lamb are good examples – and the resulting dish will be deliciously succulent.

Slow cooking, unlike microwaving and pressure cooking, is a relatively imprecise method and this turns out to be one of its greatest advantages, allowing flexible meal times for all the family. Most recipes give a minimum and a maximum cooking time to indicate the period of time at which the cooked dish is at its best. Even food that is left in the slow cooker for an hour or two longer than recommended may be past its best but will still be appreciated by hungry late-comers. Just think, no more frayed nerves when family or friends arrive late for a meal!

A slow cooker allows very little steam to escape during cooking and this has a number of benefits: the flavour of food is retained; the kitchen doesn't fill with cooking odours and steam; and water baths that would normally need topping up do not dry out.

A slow cooker can help reduce your food and fuel bills too. Nutritious meals can be cooked using inexpensive cuts of meat – the sort that demand long slow cooking to make them tender. Using a slow cooker instead of an oven can save money too. A conventional oven has a large cavity to heat up, even to cook one casserole. Inevitably, it consumes more fuel than a slow cooker, which operates at a low wattage and often using no more electricity than a light bulb. So just think, next time a light is left on all night in your home, for a similar cost you could have cooked a meal! Of course, savings will vary from model to model and on what is being cooked.

Remember too that a slow cooker heats the food inside it and not the whole kitchen (unlike a conventional oven can). On hot summer days, when the last thing we want is to spend time cooking in a hot kitchen, a slow cooker is ideal for dishes that are to be eaten hot as well as those that are to be cooled and eaten later – pâté, chilled soup, cold chicken or ham, crème caramel, pears in red wine, to name just some.

Lastly, rest assured that slow cookers are absolutely safe to leave cooking unattended all day or all night – just as you leave the fridge or freezer running while you are out. As an added guarantee of safety, slow cookers are supplied with the assurance that they meet European safety standards.

Who Uses a Slow Cooker?

Ask people why they use a slow cooker and you will be given a number of different answers, depending upon their way of life.

One-person households and particularly those with limited cooking facilities. A student in a bed-sitter for example, with perhaps only a single cooking ring, can use a slow cooker to provide healthy meals economically, at flexible times and without the neighbours complaining about lingering cooking smells.

People out at work (and that means most of us) can return home weary at the end of the day to sit down to a delicious hot meal from the slow cooker. And if they are held up at work or delayed by traffic they can be sure that the slow cooker won't burn the food or switch itself off (unlike an oven set on automatic timer). Shift workers find the slow cooker invaluable too.

Parents with young or school-age children can prepare the family meal in the morning, leaving the morning or the rest of the day free for other activities. The slow cooker can be left to cook on HIGH for lunchtime eating or on LOW for the evening. If the children prefer to eat early, that's no problem – the parents' portions can be left on LOW until they sit down to eat at a later time. Meals really can be flexible so that older children with after-school interests no longer present difficulties and there is little danger of the food spoiling before the last one arrives home.

Retired people. Whether they are home during the day or out and about, the slow cooker leaves them free to pursue their interests.

Choosing a Slow Cooker

There is a wide range of electric slow cookers on the market today and you can be sure of finding one with a shape and capacity that fits in with your lifestyle. Here are some guidelines.

Lid

The lid is usually made of glass or earthenware. With a glass lid it is possible to see what's going on inside the cooker (though condensation on the inside of the lid often obscures the view). An earthenware lid that matches the pot can look more traditional, particularly when the pot is removed from its base for serving at the table.

The lid should fit loosely on to the pot – sufficient to be able to slide it a short distance from side to side. It should however sit snugly without rocking (a lid that rocks could allow precious heat to escape from the pot). During cooking, condensation from the food gathers around the lip of the pot forming the important water seal between it and the lid (if the lid were to rock, this seal would be unlikely to form).

Pot

Slow cookers contain a cooking pot that is usually made of earthenware – an excellent insulator of heat. The capacity varies from 1.5 litres (2¾ pints) to 3.5 litres (6 pints). Some pots are narrow and deep while others are wide and shallow, depending on the location of the heat source. Pudding basins fit more easily into a deep pot but a shallow pot is better when cooking food like stuffed peppers, pears in red wine, or trout (and the larger the base, the more can be cooked at one time).

All slow cookers can be filled to within 2.5cm (1 in) of the brim without danger of boiling over. Models with a capacity of about 2.5 litres (4½ pints) are large enough for a family of four but are also suitable for cooking for one or two. Even a 1.3kg (3 lb) chicken can be cooked whole in this size. If you cook for four or more, cook for the freezer or entertain on a regular basis, I would recommend choosing a larger capacity.

There are two types of slow cooker – those with a fixed pot and those with a removable pot.

Fixed-pot Slow Cookers

It is still possible to buy a slow cooker with a pot that is permanently fixed inside it. The earthenware pot sits in an outer casing made of metal or heatproof plastic. The heating element is wrapped around the outside, between the pot and the casing. Because the heat passes from the element directly into the wall of the pot, the slow cooker uses only a small amount of electricity. Wattages vary from model to model and usually range from about 55-75 watts on LOW. So fixed-pot slow cookers are especially economical to run. Since the electrical fittings are permanently attached, the slow cooker must not be immersed in water during cleaning.

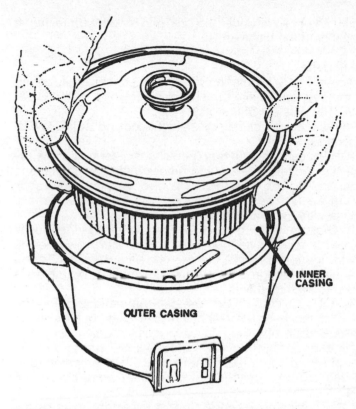

Typical slow cooker with removable stoneware pot.

Removable-pot Slow Cookers
This is the most popular type of slow cooker. The outer casing (made of metal or heatproof plastic) is fitted with an inner metal casing, into which the removable earthenware pot fits snugly. The heating element is situated in the outer casing, either in the base or around the walls. Since the heat has to be transferred through an extra layer of metal to reach the food, the electrical consumption is slightly higher – about 80-105 watts on LOW – and still extremely economical. It's more versatile that the fixed-pot model because the earthenware container can be lifted out of its base to serve at table,

to put in the oven or under the grill, and to wash up (either at the sink or in the dishwasher).

Heat Settings

Settings will vary slightly between slow cookers but, generally, the best ones have three cooking settings (LOW, HIGH and AUTO) plus an OFF switch.

LOW is ideal for all-day or all-night cooking at the lowest temperature.

HIGH is useful to speed up cooking, say for lunchtime, by increasing the temperature and reducing the cooking time to almost half that on LOW. HIGH is also used to cook foods that require fast heat penetration, such as joints of meat, whole poultry, pâté and steamed puddings.

AUTO starts cooking on HIGH then, when the thermostat indicates a specific temperature, automatically switches to LOW for the remainder of the cooking period – useful if you are adding cold ingredients to the slow cooker or if there is no time to preheat it first.

It is not possible to relate the cooking settings on a slow cooker to those on an electric or gas oven but it's worth knowing that the cooking liquid in a slow cooker rises to a temperature around 100°C (boiling point) – hot enough to cook the food thoroughly and safely. This temperature is achieved on both settings but is reached more quickly on HIGH.

At the beginning of cooking it is important to raise the temperature as quickly as possible to destroy any harmful bacteria that may be present. This can be achieved in several ways and you should always follow the manufacturer's own instructions for your particular model. One method is to preheat the slow cooker on HIGH for about 20 minutes while you prepare the ingredients. Another is to bring all the ingredients to boiling point before adding them to the slow cooker, and yet another is to use the AUTO setting.

Indicator Lights

Most slow cookers are fitted with an indicator light to show that they are switched on in use. This is particularly useful because a slow cooker heats up slowly and, without an indicator light, it is possible to leave the house thinking that the slow cooker is switched on, when, in fact, the plug may not have been pushed in properly. It's not funny returning home to a pot full of uncooked food!

Flex and Plug

A detachable flex is convenient, allowing the slow cooker to be taken to the table and to be cleaned easily (particularly if it has a fixed pot).

Most slow cookers come with a fitted plug containing the correct fuse. If, for some reason, you need to fit a new plug or replace the fuse, it is important to follow the instructions given by the manufacturer of your slow cooker.

Do not be tempted to fit a time switch to switch on the slow cooker in your absence. It is not safe to leave food at room temperature in ideal conditions for bacteria growth.

The Decision

When choosing a slow cooker, first decide which capacity you need. Allow a little extra capacity if you entertain or cook for the freezer. Next decide whether you need a slow cooker with a fixed pot or a removable pot – the latter is generally a little more expensive.

Finally, before buying, read through the instruction book provided by the manufacturer and check that it gives you a wide range of recipes with cooking methods that suit your lifestyle.

Using a Slow Cooker

Slow cookers do differ slightly so, for best results, it is important to follow your manufacturer's basic instructions.

Check whether they recommend preheating the slow cooker on HIGH while the ingredients are being prepared.

Check whether you should then keep the food on HIGH for a time before switching to LOW. If this is the case, you should do it as a matter of course, even though I have not mentioned it in my recipes in this book (the cooking times will remain approximately the same).

Preparation

Using a slow cooker requires a certain amount of forethought but, once you have devised your own method of preparation, slow cooking will become automatic. I have developed my own pattern of preparation that I hope you will find useful, especially if, like me, you are short of time in the morning.

- Assemble the ingredients the previous evening.

- If the meat is still in the freezer, remove first and prepare last, allowing it time to thaw partially at room temperature.

- Peel any root vegetables. Peel and chop onions. Store in sealed containers or bags in the fridge.

- Into a shallow bowl, measure out any flour to be used for thickening, add the required seasoning, mix well and cover.

- Trim meat of excess fat and cut to the required size. Even if the meat is still frozen and too hard to cut, it may still be possible to trim off the fat (it's often easier to remove while still partly frozen). Cover the meat and store overnight in the fridge.

- Do not store uncooked food in the slow cooker either at room temperature or in the fridge. In the first instance, the food could go off and in the second, the slow cooker could be damaged when the cold surfaces come into contact with the heat.

- The next morning, if preheating is recommended, switch the slow cooker to HIGH as soon as you arrive in the kitchen.

- Remove the ingredients from the fridge and, if you need to dissolve a stock cube, put the kettle on to boil. Chop the root vegetables and, if necessary, cut the meat.

There are two basic ways of preparing a savoury recipe: the Browning Method and the One-step Method.

The Browning Method
Browning certainly improves the flavour and appearance of many recipes. Some people, however, prefer not to bother with this additional process and it really is a matter of individual taste. This method is not suitable for fish.

1. Switch the slow cooker on HIGH.

2. Heat a little fat or oil in a large deep frying pan. A non-stick pan requires little or no fat.

3. To the hot pan, add the prepared flavouring vegetables (such as onion, celery, potato, carrot or celeriac), and cook over a medium heat for about 5 minutes, stirring

occasionally, until softened and just starting to brown. Using a slotted spoon, transfer to the slow cooker.

4. If you prefer a thickened soup or casserole, toss the pieces of meat in flour. Add to the hot pan and brown quickly all over. When browning a joint, turn on all sides for even colour. Using a slotted spoon, transfer the browned meat to the slow cooker.

5. Sprinkle the herbs and seasoning over the food in the slow cooker and pour in the hot cooking liquid. (Alternatively, if you are using a deep frying pan or large saucepan, you could leave the vegetables and meat in the pan and add herbs, seasoning and liquid. Bring everything to the boil, stirring, until the flour has thickened the sauce.)

6. Put the lid on, switch to LOW and cook for the recommended time.

The One-step Method
Use this method if you are short of time, if you want to use less fat, or if you simply prefer not to brown the food first.

1. Switch the slow cooker on HIGH.

2. Make sure that vegetables such as onions, carrots, potatoes, celery and celeriac are cut small and put into the slow cooker first.

3. Add the meat or skinless poultry.

4. Add herbs and seasoning and pour over sufficient hot cooking liquid to barely cover the food, making sure that the vegetables are immersed.

5. Put the lid on, switch to LOW and cook for the minimum recommended time plus 2-3 hours.

Cooking Settings and Times – Guidelines
●   Once the food has been put into the slow cooker, select the setting that suits your day.

●   Recipes usually recommend minimum and maximum

cooking times on LOW but you may prefer to cook on HIGH.

- Calculate the time on HIGH as just over half that on LOW.

- There are certain foods that will need to be cooked on HIGH throughout and you will need to check with your manufacturer's instruction book. Steamed puddings that include a raising agent are generally cooked on HIGH (to ensure the mixture rises well), as are meat pâtés, whole birds and some joints of meat (to ensure speedy and thorough heat penetration and the destruction of any harmful bacteria present).

- Some foods are not suitable for cooking all day, including fish, pasta, rice and most desserts.

- Slow cookers operate slightly differently from model to model. Use the cooking times in my recipes as a guide and don't be afraid to adjust them slightly to suit your slow cooker. It's a good idea to compare cooking times in my recipes with similar ones in your manufacturer's instruction booklet. I suggest you start by checking Mixed Vegetable Soup (page 34), Irish Stew (page 74) and Chicken and Mushroom Casserole (page 85). These comparisons will help you to decide whether you should increase or reduce the cooking time in your slow cooker (or indeed leave it as it is).

During Cooking
- Once the lid has been put on the slow cooker, it is best to forget about it until shortly before you are ready to serve the food. Resist the temptation to lift the lid and peep during cooking – you will only break the water seal around the rim and release heat. For the first hour, the slow cooker works hard, heating up its contents to a temperature at which they will cook. So if heat is lost during this early stage of cooking you will need to lengthen the cooking time considerably. For each lid-lifting peep during the first half of cooking, you will need to add approximately 20 minutes to the cooking time. So, unless the recipe states otherwise, limit stirring to the final stages of cooking.

- Make sure that the slow cooker stands on a heat-resistant surface during cooking as the heat from the base could harm a highly polished surface such as a dining table. Also, when cooking on HIGH, the slow cooker may 'spit' very small amounts of hot liquid from the edge of the lid. This simply indicates a slight build-up of pressure that is venting through the water seal and is no cause for alarm (though it will not do your polished table any good).

- Extreme room conditions are likely to affect the performance of a slow cooker. So do keep yours out of cold draughts or you may need to extend the cooking time as much as an hour.

After Cooking
- The slow cooker will continue cooking until it is switched off at the plug.

- If some of the food is to be kept for a latecomer, leave the slow cooker switched on and set at LOW.

- If some of the food is to be kept for another day, the extra portions should be removed from the slow cooker as soon as it is switched off, transferred to a clean container and cooled quickly before refrigerating or freezing.

- Never leave food to cool slowly in the slow cooker as earthenware retains heat for long periods.

- Do not use your slow cooker to reheat cold or frozen food – the temperature rise is too slow (Christmas pudding is the only exception to this rule). Instead, put the cold food into a pan and bring to the boil on the hob.

Adapting Recipes for Slow Cooking
The simplest way to adapt one of your own recipes is to find one with similar ingredients in this book. This will give you a basic guide to the quantities, method and cooking times. Remember that the ingredients that take longest to cook (such as carrots, potatoes and dried beans) will dictate the cooking time. If in doubt, you can always contact the manufacturer of your slow cooker for advice. In the meantime, the following points are worth bearing in mind:

Frozen Ingredients

All frozen fish, meat, poultry and game must be thawed completely before cooking, otherwise the slow cooker will not reach safe cooking temperatures and food will be undercooked. Frozen vegetables, such as peas, beans and sweetcorn, should be thawed and added during the final 30 minutes of cooking.

Vegetables

Though it seems odd, most vegetables take longer to cook than meat. This is because the temperature needed for meat to begin cooking is lower than that required by vegetables.

To encourage vegetables (such as onions, celery, root vegetables and potatoes) to get hot fast, they should be cut into small dice or sliced thinly. Put the vegetables in the hottest part of the pot – in other words, on the bottom or towards the sides, depending on where the element is situated. Always make sure they are completely immersed in the liquid during cooking. Finally, it helps to speed things up if vegetables are softened or browned in a pan first and then brought up to the boil before putting them in the slow cooker.

Flavour

Loss of liquid through evaporation is kept to a minimum in the slow cooker. Hence the juices are concentrated and the flavour is retained. Take care not to use too many herbs and strong-flavoured vegetables until you achieve the balance of flavour that suits you.

Cooking Liquid

This can be water, stock, wine, beer, cider or fruit juice, and soups (canned, dried or condensed) can be useful too.

You'll find that you need less liquid than in conventional cooking. Not only is there less evaporation, but also the juices from the meat and vegetables are conserved in the stock. Consequently you are usually left with more liquid than you started with. This is particularly noticeable when using condensed soups – when it is first put into the slow cooker, the soup is thick and lumpy but, after cooking, the juices can be stirred in to give a smooth sauce (don't add seasoning to condensed soup as it is usually strongly seasoned already).

Packet soups are useful for making a quick basis for a

Root vegetables should be cut small for thorough cooking. Onions, for instance, should be halved, then cut first lengthways then crossways.

casserole and should be prepared using half the recommended amount of water. Canned 'cook-in' sauces can be used with great success too.

Except when adding them to milk puddings, cream and milk should not be used for long slow cooking because they tend to separate. Milk is best added during the final 30 minutes' cooking; cream is best stirred in just before serving.

Thickening
Juices from the meat and vegetables tend to make a thin sauce, so it is important to start cooking with a sauce that is thicker than usual.

When using the Browning Method, toss the meat in flour before frying. Alternatively, flour or cornflour may be blended with a little cold water to make a smooth pouring cream and added to the cooking liquid before it is brought to the boil, stirring continuously, until thickened.

In the One-step Method, the best way to thicken a sauce is to switch the slow cooker to HIGH for the final 30 minutes and stir in some cornflour that has been blended with a little cold water.

Pasta
Pasta that is cooked too long becomes unpleasantly soft. So add it to the slow cooker during the final 30 minutes' cooking. When making lasagne, either use fresh pasta or soften dried lasagne sheets in boiling water until soft first. To make sure it cooks evenly and throughout, pasta should always be totally immersed in the sauce during cooking.

Rice
Easy-cook long grain rice produces best results in the slow cooker. When rice features as the main ingredient, as in Savoury Rice with Rosemary (page 117) or Chicken Risotto (page 93), it should be stirred a couple of times during cooking to ensure even absorption of liquid. When cooking a casserole or soup for several hours or all day, add the rice for the final 30 minutes. Remember, rice will absorb some of the liquid so allow an extra 150ml (¼ pint) for each 55g (2 oz) rice.

Dried Beans
Dried beans need soaking overnight in plenty of cold water before slow cooking. Alternatively, boil them in plenty of water for 2 minutes, allow them to soak (in the water in which they were boiled) for 2 hours and then drain.

Because the cooking times vary so much (according to the type, size and age of the beans), at this stage I like to bring them to the boil in clean water for 10 minutes before draining and putting into the slow cooker. Red kidney beans should **always** be fast-boiled for 10 minutes before draining and transferring to the slow cooker – to destroy their toxins.

Lentils do not need soaking before cooking – just put them straight into the slow cooker.

Season dried beans after cooking, as salt tends to toughen the skins.

Toppings
If the earthenware pot is removable, you can add toppings to the cooked food and put the pot into the oven or under the grill to finish cooking.

- Pipe mashed potato over a cooked casserole and bake quickly in a hot oven until browned.

- Sprinkle with grated cheese and brown under a hot grill.

- Make a scone topping and bake in the oven (Beef Cobbler, page 62).

- Top slices of French bread with grated cheese or spread them with French mustard. Arrange the slices on top of a soup or casserole and brown under a hot grill.

- Add a layer of a crumble mixture to cooked fruit and bake in the oven.

- Pile meringue on to cooked fruit and bake in the oven (see Fragrant Rhubarb Meringue on page 126).

Not Quite Right? Troubleshooting Guide

Slow cooking, like any new method of cooking, needs a bit of practice before you feel at home with it. Don't be discouraged if your first attempt isn't quite right. Even the most experienced cook has to adapt techniques slightly. Try to discover what went wrong and, if in doubt, contact the manufacturer who often has experts on hand to answer queries. In the meantime, here are some of the more common problems experienced, together with possible answers.

The food was put into the slow cooker but, at the end of the recommended cooking time, was cold and uncooked.
Was the plug pushed properly into the slow cooker? Could it have been knocked out during cooking? Check the fuse in the plug.

The food didn't cook in the recommended time.
With the One-step Method, did you add 2-3 hours to the minimum recommended time? Did you add *hot* liquid? Is the slow cooker standing in a cold draught? Does the lid fit well, lying perfectly flat on the rim of the pot? If you cooked on LOW, next time try AUTO.

The meat was cooked but the vegetables were still crunchy.
Were the vegetables cut small enough? Were they immersed in the liquid? Next time, put them in the base of the pot with

the other ingredients on top; or soften them first in a little oil or butter in a pan on the hob.

The gravy or sauce was too thin.
Use less liquid than you would in a conventional recipe. Alternatively, add extra thickening at the beginning or end of cooking.

The casserole is sometimes brown and 'crusty' on top after 10 hours' cooking.
It may not look appetising but it tastes good, so stir it into the casserole before serving. Next time, try adding a little extra liquid.

The potatoes have turned black and are uncooked.
Were they protruding above the liquid? Next time, make sure they are fully immersed.

The vegetables have cooked but the meat is still tough.
Some meat just takes a long time to tenderise. Next time you use this cut, cut the vegetables slightly larger and cook the dish for 1-2 hours longer.

There is an odd smell when the slow cooker is operating.
When new plastic insulation and fittings are heated for the first few times, they can smell slightly. This should disappear. However, if the smell persists, contact the manufacturer.

You arrive home early and the meal isn't yet ready.
Switch the slow cooker to HIGH to speed up the cooking.

Extra Equipment
Using the appropriate equipment makes cooking a lot easier. I have found the following items invaluable when slow cooking.

For browning meat and softening vegetables, I recommend a *deep non-stick frying pan* or saucepan with a thick base. This will allow you to brown with little or no added fat.

Use *a slotted spoon* to transfer browned meat or vegetables from the frying pan to the slow cooker (to leave excess fat behind in the pan).

A set of *measuring spoons* ensures that you add the correct measure of herbs, seasoning, thickening, whatever.

When cooking puddings, pâtés or cakes, ensure that your

Deep non-stick frying pan ideal for pre-browning.

basins and tins fit inside the slow cooker without raising the lid. Some slow cookers have a lid that is slightly domed and it is surprising how large a basin will fit beneath. A 1 litre (1¾ pint) basin may be too big for some smaller slow cookers, while a soufflé dish of the same capacity may fit easily.

Lifting strap on pudding basin.

If the container fits so snugly that it is difficult to lift out, make a *lifting strap*. Cut a 60cm (2 ft) length of 30cm (1 ft) wide foil and fold in half lengthways. Fold it in half again to make a strap 60cm (2 ft) long and 7.5cm (3 in) wide. Pass the strap under the container, hold both ends tightly together and lift the container into the slow cooker. Leave in position during cooking and use the strap to lift the hot container from the slow cooker. After use, the strap can be dried and used again.

A *blender* or a *food processor* is invaluable when preparing soups.

Care and Cleaning

The most vulnerable part of the slow cooker is the earthenware pot, which will break if dropped and chip if knocked hard. For the same reason earthenware and glass lids should be handled with care.

Sudden changes in temperature are also likely to damage the earthenware pot. For this reason, it should not be put into the freezer or fridge and you should avoid placing it on any surface that is very hot or very cold (instead, stand it on a thick cloth or a wooden chopping board). The outer casing should not be preheated empty before adding the cold pot. Frozen food should be thawed completely before adding to the slow cooker. When adding water before leaving the pot to soak, it is better to use warm or hot water rather than cold.

Always use oven gloves to remove a hot earthenware pot from the slow cooker.

Always remove the pot from the outer casing before grilling or oven cooking. A slow cooker with a fixed pot, or a lid with plastic fittings, should never be put into a hot oven – the heat will melt the plastic and cause dangerous electrical damage. For the same reason, don't be tempted to store the slow cooker in a cold oven – it's so easy to forget it is there when you next switch on the oven.

Do not put food or liquid straight into the outer casing.

Slow cookers create such relatively low temperatures that it is rare to find a burnt-on tidemark around the edge of the pot – the sort that is common with oven-cooked dishes. As a result, the earthenware pot, whether fixed or removable, is not difficult to clean.

After serving, switch off the slow cooker and, if you don't plan to wash it immediately, fill with hot or warm water. Pour away this soaking water just before you clean the pot.

A removable pot can be lifted out of the casing and washed in a dishwasher, or in a bowl of hot soapy water using a nylon scrubber or brush. A slow cooker with fixed pot should not be immersed in the water but should be stood on the draining board. If the flex is detachable, remove it; otherwise keep the plug away from the water. Half fill the pot with hot soapy water and clean using a nylon scrubber or brush. Pour away this water, fill with clean rinsing water, pour away and dry.

Sometimes, a white chalky deposit marks the pot after steaming a pudding. This should be removed with a nylon, not metal, scourer and a mild liquid cleaner.

Wipe the exterior with a damp cloth. The inner lining may also be wiped if the pot is removable, but remember that the metal may still be hot. Take care not to let food spill out of the pot into the outer casing, as it will burn on. Never put water into the outer casing.

On no account try to repair an electrical fault yourself. The manufacturer is best equipped to do the job safely and efficiently.

2

SOUPS

How about a pot of homemade soup simmering away, ready to greet you and your family or friends when you get home? With a slow cooker, making soup is really convenient – and it can be economical too.

I like to make soups from whatever I have to hand. Most store cupboards contain the ingredients for a nourishing soup. Lentil Soup, for example, is simply prepared with dried lentils, onions, a can of tomatoes and a stock cube. Use seasonal vegetables or a glut from the garden to make delicious soups, such as Broccoli Soup (page 38). Eat some now and freeze some for another time; or indeed freeze all of it for an out-of-season treat.

Why not save vegetable peelings, bones or poultry

carcasses as a matter of course? Then follow the recipe for Stock on page 31 and you will have an excellent basis for future soups or casseroles, at virtually no cost.

Soups can be oooked all day or overnight. They generally need at least 8 hours on LOW and most soups can be left for 12 hours without danger of overcooking. Because soups often involve lengthy preparation, you may find it more convenient to cut up the ingredients during the evening and cook overnight. Or why not prepare the ingredients the previous evening and cook the peelings or bones overnight to make the stock for the next day's soup? By making your own stock you will make soups with a flavour that is more subtle than that made with a stock cube (most of which tend to be strongly flavoured).

For a light meal, serve soup as a main dish. Minestrone (page 36) and Dutch Cabbage Soup with Smoked Sausage (page 37), for example, need only a chunk of fresh crusty bread to complete the meal.

If you have a really large slow cooker, it's often worth doubling the quantities and freezing the extra portions. Even if your slow cooker is small, you can make large amounts of soup by doubling the solid ingredients and oooking them with the single quantity of liquid. The cooking time will be the same. Then, freeze the soup in its condensed state (in single or double portions) and simply dilute it when you reheat it.

To convert your own recipes, follow the basic method below.

1. Preheat the slow cooker on HIGH if necessary.

2. Assemble the ingredients and prepare as usual, cutting root vegetables into small dice.

3. Heat a little oil or butter in a large saucepan, add the vegetables and cook, stirring occasionally, until softened but not browned. (Alternatively, omit the fat and simply put the vegetables in the pan.)

4. Add any meat and brown quickly on all sides. If you are not adding fat, you will need to use a non-stick pan.

5. For 4-6 servings, add approximately 1 litre (1¾ pints) stock or water.

6. Bring everything to the boil and, if necessary, use a slotted spoon to remove any scum from the surface.

    To thicken the soup, blend 1-2 tablespoonfuls corn-flour with sufficient water to make a smooth pouring cream, add to the pan and bring to the boil, stirring continuously, until thickened.

7. Add herbs (dried herbs give a good flavour) and seasoning.

8. Transfer to the slow cooker, put the lid on and cook on LOW for 8-12 hours or on HIGH for 4-6 hours.

9. If necessary, cut the meat off the bones and discard the bones. Adjust the seasoning to taste if necessary.

10. Some soups benefit from liquidising in a blender or puréeing in a food processor. Alternatively, you may prefer a chunky texture – the choice is yours. Soup that is liquidised can either be returned to the slow cooker and reheated on HIGH for 15 minutes or reheated in a saucepan on the hob.

11. Soups can be made more luxurious by stirring in extra ingredients at the end of cooking – a beaten egg yolk, cream or milk can be stirred in about 15 minutes before serving (do not add it earlier as it is likely to curdle).

12. Adding a last-minute garnish can make a soup more appealing and fresh-tasting. Just before serving, stir in or sprinkle with chopped fresh herbs or spring onions, grated cheese, crisp croûtons or crisp-cooked bacon pieces; or swirl in a little double cream, soured cream or natural yoghurt.

Stock

Homemade stock is a real treat. Let it simmer away overnight in the slow cooker. If you don't want to use it immediately, freeze the cooled stock in small quantities and use within a month.

LOW 10-14 hours

**raw or cooked beef, lamb or chicken bones, broken into small pieces
selection of vegetables (or their scrubbed peelings) such as carrot, turnip, leek and celery, thinly sliced
1 onion, finely chopped
a few bacon rinds (optional)
bouquet garni
6 peppercorns**

1. Preheat the slow cooker on HIGH.

2. Place all the ingredients in the pot and pour over sufficient boiling water to cover.

3. Put the lid on and cook on LOW for 10-14 hours.

4. Strain the stock then cool completely and refrigerate.

5. Before using, remove any fat that has solidified on the surface. Use within 2 days.

Chicken Broth with Mushrooms and Barley

Here is a soup that could hardly be simpler to make. If you have some, stir in some chopped fresh parsley, tarragon or chives just before serving.

Serves 4-6   *LOW 6-10 hours*

**4 boneless chicken thighs, skin removed, trimmed and
   cut into small pieces
1 medium onion, finely chopped
25g (1 oz) pearl barley
115g (4 oz) mushrooms, sliced
½ tsp mixed dried herbs
1 litre (1¾ pints) boiling chicken stock
salt and freshly milled pepper**

1.   Preheat the slow cooker on HIGH.

2.   Put all the ingredients into the slow cooker.

3.   Put the lid on and cook on LOW for 6-10 hours.

4.   Adjust the seasoning to taste before serving.

Creamy Celery Soup

In my opinion, chicken stock gives the best flavour to this soup though you may prefer to replace it with vegetable stock. If you plan to freeze the soup, omit the cream and add it to the thawed mixture before reheating.

Serves 4-6   *LOW 6-10 hours*

25g (1 oz) butter
1 medium onion, finely chopped
1 head of celery, thinly sliced
2 tbsp plain flour
850ml (1½ pints) chicken stock
150ml (¼ pint) double cream
salt and freshly milled pepper

1. Preheat the slow cooker on HIGH.

2. Meanwhile, heat the butter in a large saucepan, add the onion and celery and cook gently, stirring occasionally, until softened but not browned.

3. Stir in the flour. Remove from the heat and gradually stir in the stock.

4. Bring to the boil, stirring continuously, and transfer to the slow cooker.

5. Put the lid on and cook on LOW for 6-10 hours.

6. Liquidise or process the soup until smooth (you may need to do this in batches).

7. Add the cream and heat through, seasoning with salt and pepper to taste.

Mixed Vegetable Soup

Vary your choice of vegetables to suit the season. Hot garlic bread makes a delicious accompaniment.

Serves 4-6   *LOW 6-10 hours*

25g (1 oz) butter
2 large onions, finely chopped
5 medium carrots, finely diced
3 turnips, finely diced
3 medium potatoes, finely diced
1 green pepper, seeds removed, diced
850ml (1½ pints) chicken stock
2 tbsp plain flour
400g can tomatoes
2 tbsp tomato purée
2 bay leaves
salt and freshly milled pepper

1. Preheat the slow cooker on HIGH.

2. Meanwhile, heat the butter in a large saucepan, add the onions and cook gently, stirring occasionally, until softened but not browned.

3. Add the carrots, turnips, potatoes and green pepper and cook gently for 3-4 minutes, stirring occasionally.

4. Add the stock.

5. Blend the flour with a little of the tomato juice to make a smooth pouring cream. Add to the soup with the rest of the tomatoes, the tomato purée and bay leaves. Bring to the boil, stirring continuously.

6. Put the lid on and cook on LOW for 6-10 hours.

7. Remove the bay leaves before serving and season to taste.

Vichysoisse

Traditionally, Vichysoisse is made using only the white or palest green part of the leeks (keep the dark green leaves to flavour a casserole). Make sure you remove all traces of soil from the leeks – by slicing them thinly into a colander and washing thoroughly under cold running water.

Serves 6   *LOW 6-10 hours*

25g (1 oz) butter
450g (1 lb) potatoes, diced small
1kg (2 lb 4 oz) leeks, thinly sliced – see above
850ml (1½ pints) chicken stock
300ml (½ pint) milk or single cream
salt and white pepper
chopped fresh chives, to serve

1.   Preheat the slow cooker on HIGH.

2.   Meanwhile, heat the butter in a large saucepan, add the potatoes and cook gently for about 3 minutes, stirring occasionally, without browning.

3.   Add the leeks and cook for 2 minutes, stirring occasionally, without browning.

4.   Add the stock, bring to the boil and transfer to the slow cooker.

5.   Put the lid on and cook on LOW for 6-10 hours.

6.   Liquidise or process the soup until smooth (you may need to do this in batches) and transfer to a large bowl.

7.   Stir in the milk or cream, season to taste with salt and pepper and refrigerate until cold.

8.   Serve chilled, sprinkled with chopped chives.

Minestrone

Served with crusty bread, this soup makes a substantial snack or lunch.

Serves 4-6   *LOW 6-8 hours*

1 tbsp oil
2 lean bacon rashers, finely chopped
1 medium onion, finely chopped
2 medium carrots, grated or finely diced
1 leek, thinly sliced
2 celery sticks, thinly sliced
115g (4 oz) white cabbage, finely shredded
1 garlic clove, crushed
1 litre (1¾ pints) chicken stock
4 tbsp tomato purée
400g can tomatoes
bouquet garni
salt and freshly milled black pepper
55g (2 oz) short macaroni
freshly grated Parmesan cheese

1.   Preheat the slow cooker on HIGH.

2.   Heat the oil in a large saucepan, add the bacon and cook, stirring occasionally, until it starts to brown.

3.   Add the onion, carrots, leek, celery, cabbage and garlic. Cook gently for 3-4 minutes, stirring occasionally.

4.   Add the stock, tomato purée, tomatoes, bouquet garni and a little seasoning. Bring to the boil and transfer to the slow cooker.

5.   Put the lid on and cook for 6-8 hours on LOW, stirring in the macaroni for the final ½-1 hour.

6.   Remove the bouquet garni and adjust the seasoning to taste. Serve sprinkled with grated Parmesan.

Dutch Cabbage Soup with Smoked Sausage

A Dutch pork sausage is approximately 30cm (12 in) long and curled into a horseshoe shape. For slow cookers with a capacity of 2 litres (3½ pints) or less, you may need to reduce the quantity of cabbage in this recipe.

Serves 4-6   *LOW 7-10 hours*

1 small or half a large white cabbage, finely shredded
1 medium onion, finely chopped
227g Dutch smoked sausage, skinned and cut into 1cm
(½ in) slices
1 litre (1¾ pints) boiling chicken stock
salt and freshly milled pepper

1.   Preheat the slow cooker on HIGH.

2.   Put the cabbage, onion and sausage into the slow cooker and pour the boiling stock over.

3.   Stir well, and then push the ingredients below the surface of the liquid.

4.   Put the lid on and cook on LOW for 7-10 hours.

Broccoli Soup

Delicious served with a little blue cheese (such as Stilton) crumbled over the top. The evaporated milk could be replaced with single cream.

Serves 4-6   *LOW 5-8 hours*

25g (1 oz) butter
1 medium onion, finely chopped
450g (1 lb) small broccoli florets
850ml (1½ pints) chicken stock
½ tsp finely grated nutmeg
170g can evaporated milk
salt and freshly milled pepper

1. Preheat the slow cooker on HIGH.

2. Meanwhile, heat the butter in a large saucepan, add the onion and cook gently, stirring occasionally, until softened but not browned.

3. Stir in the broccoli, stock and nutmeg. Bring to the boil and transfer to the slow cooker.

4. Put the lid on and cook on LOW for 5-8 hours.

5. Liquidise or process the soup (you may need to do this in batches).

6. Add the milk, season to taste and heat through gently without boiling.

Scotch Broth

This recipe, also known in Scotland as Barley Broth, traditionally calls for mutton. Since this is not so easy to find today, I use lamb instead.

Serves 4-6   *LOW 7-9 hours*

**225g (8 oz) middle neck of lamb (weight after being
   trimmed of excess fat)**
1 litre (1¾ pints) lamb stock
1 medium onion, finely chopped
2 medium carrots, grated or finely diced
1 medium potato, grated or finely diced
55g (2 oz) pearl barley
bouquet garni
salt and freshly milled black pepper

1. Preheat the slow cooker on HIGH.

2. Meanwhile, cut the lamb from the bones and chop into small pieces.

3. Put the lamb, bones and stock into a large saucepan and bring to the boil. Skim the surface.

4. Add the remaining ingredients, bring back to the boil and transfer to the slow cooker.

5. Put the lid on and cook on LOW for 7-9 hours.

6. Before serving, remove and discard the bouquet garni. Lift the bones out, remove any meat still clinging to them and add to the soup. Adjust seasoning to taste.

Oxtail Soup

Oxtail has masses of flavour and really benefits from long, slow cooking. Sometimes, I stir in a little sherry to this soup just before serving.

Serves 4-6   *LOW 8-12 hours*

1 tbsp oil
6-8 oxtail pieces, trimmed of excess fat
1 large onion, finely chopped
2 medium carrots, thinly sliced
1 litre (1¾ pints) beef stock
2 tbsp plain flour
2 tbsp tomato purée
1 tsp paprika
bouquet garni
salt and freshly milled black pepper

1. Preheat the slow cooker on HIGH.

2. Heat the oil in a large saucepan, add the oxtail and cook, turning occasionally, until browned all over. Lift out and put to one side. Pour away excess fat, leaving about 1 tbsp in the pan.

3. Add the onion and carrots to the hot fat and cook, stirring occasionally, until softened but not browned.

4. Add the browned oxtail pieces and the stock.

5. Blend the flour with a little cold water to make a smooth pouring cream. Add to the pan and bring to the boil, stirring continuously, until thickened.

6. Transfer to the slow cooker and stir in the remaining ingredients.

7. Put the lid on and cook on LOW for 8-12 hours.

8. Remove and discard the bouquet garni. Lift out the oxtail pieces, pick the meat from the bones and add to the soup. Adjust the seasoning to taste before serving.

Red Lentil Soup

Lentils do not need soaking before slow cooking. This soup is good served with fresh granary bread and mature Cheddar cheese.

Serves 4-6   *LOW 6-10 hours*

4 streaky bacon rashers, finely chopped
1 medium onion, finely chopped
1 small carrot, finely chopped
115g (4 oz) red lentils
400g can tomatoes
½ tsp dried mixed herbs
850ml (1½ pints) chicken stock
salt and freshly milled pepper

1. Preheat the slow cooker on HIGH.

2. In a large non-stick saucepan, heat the bacon until the fat begins to run. Add the onion and carrot and cook gently, stirring occasionally, until golden brown.

3. Add the remaining ingredients and bring to the boil. Simmer gently for 5 minutes and transfer to the slow cooker.

4. Put the lid on and cook on LOW for 6-10 hours.

5. Adjust the seasoning to taste and serve. Alternatively, liquidise or process the soup until smooth (you may need to do this in batches) and heat through.

Watercress and Potato Soup

Crisp croûtons go well with this peppery soup.

Serves 4-6   *LOW 5-9 hours*

25g (1 oz) butter
1 medium onion, finely chopped
2 large potatoes, finely diced
1 bunch of watercress, including stalks, chopped
1 garlic clove, crushed (optional)
1 litre (1¾ pints) hot chicken stock
salt and freshly milled black pepper
single cream, to serve

1. Heat the butter in a large saucepan, add the onion and cook gently, stirring occasionally, until softened but not browned.

2. Stir in the potatoes and watercress and cook gently for 1-2 minutes, stirring occasionally.

3. Add the remaining ingredients, except the cream, and bring to the boil. Transfer to the slow cooker.

4. Put the lid on and cook on LOW for 5-9 hours.

5. Liquidise or process the soup (you may need to do this in batches) until smooth. Adjust the seasoning to taste and heat through.

6. To serve, swirl a little cream on top of each serving.

Cock-a-Leekie

If wished, the meat may be cut from the bones the previous evening and the bones may be used to cook the stock overnight.

Serves 4-6   *LOW 6-10 hours*

4 boneless chicken thighs, skin removed, trimmed and cut into small pieces
1 medium onion, finely chopped
450g (1 lb) leeks, thinly sliced
8 dried prunes, stones removed, roughly chopped
1 litre (1¾ pints) boiling chicken stock
salt and freshly milled pepper

1. Preheat the slow cooker on HIGH.

2. Put all the ingredients into the slow cooker and stir well.

3. Put the lid on and cook on LOW for 6-10 hours.

Spiced Beef Soup

All your favourite curry ingredients make up this soup. Choose mild, medium or hot curry powder – to suit your taste. Serve with crisp croûtons.

Serves 4-6   *LOW 7-10 hours*

1 tbsp oil
1 medium onion, finely chopped
2 celery sticks, thinly sliced
450g (1 lb) lean stewing beef, cut into small cubes
2 tbsp plain flour
1 tbsp curry powder
1 tsp ground ginger
1 tbsp mango chutney
1 garlic clove, crushed
2 tbsp tomato purée
1 litre (1¾ pints) beef stock
1 tbsp lemon juice
salt and freshly milled black pepper

1. Preheat the slow cooker on HIGH.

2. Meanwhile, heat the oil in a large saucepan, add the onion and celery and cook gently, stirring occasionally, until golden brown.

3. Add the beef and cook for 3-4 minutes, stirring occasionally.

4. Stir in the flour, curry powder and ginger.

5. Add the chutney, garlic and tomato purée, stirring until well mixed.

6. Remove from the heat and gradually stir in the stock. Bring to the boil and transfer to the slow cooker.

7. Put the lid on and cook on LOW for 7-10 hours, stirring in the lemon juice and adjusting the seasoning to taste about 15 minutes before serving.

Goulash Soup

Like the Hungarian dish called Goulash, this soup is good topped with a dollop of soured cream and a sprinkling of paprika.

Serves 4-6   *LOW 7-10 hours*

450g (1 lb) lean minced beef
2 medium onions, finely chopped
2 tbsp plain flour
2 tbsp paprika
½ tsp grated nutmeg
2 tbsp tomato purée
2 garlic cloves, crushed
1 litre (1¾ pints) beef stock
2 bay leaves
salt and freshly milled black pepper

1. Preheat the slow cooker on HIGH.

2. In a large non-stick saucepan, gently cook the beef, stirring frequently, until any fat begins to run out.

3. Add the onions and cook, stirring occasionally, until the beef is browned and the onions have softened.

4. Stir in the flour, paprika and nutmeg.

5. Add the remaining ingredients and bring to the boil, stirring continuously. Transfer to the slow cooker.

6. Put the lid on and cook on LOW for 7-10 hours.

7. Remove the bay leaves and adjust seasoning to taste before serving.

Cream of Spinach Soup with Nutmeg

Spinach and nutmeg have flavours that complement each other well. Though I prefer to use chicken stock, you may prefer to use vegetable.

Serves 4-6   *LOW 4-6 hours*

25g (1 oz) butter
1 medium onion, finely chopped
225g (8 oz) frozen chopped spinach, thawed
½ tsp grated nutmeg
850ml (1½ pints) chicken stock
3-4 tbsp crème fraîche
salt and freshly milled black pepper
freshly grated Parmesan cheese

1. Preheat the slow cooker on HIGH.

2. Heat the butter in a large saucepan, add the onion and cook gently, stirring occasionally, until softened but not browned.

3. Add the spinach, nutmeg and stock. Bring to the boil and transfer to the slow cooker.

4. Put the lid on and cook on LOW for 4-6 hours, stirring in the crème fraîche for the final 20-30 minutes.

5. Season to taste with salt and black pepper. Serve sprinkled with Parmesan cheese.

Mediterranean Fish Soup

I like to buy a selection of different fish to make up the required quantity.

Serves 4-6   *LOW 3-6 hours*

2 tbsp olive oil
2 medium onions, finely chopped
2 leeks, finely chopped
227g can chopped tomatoes
2 garlic cloves, crushed
1 litre (1¾ pints) fish stock or water
bay leaf
bouquet garni
finely grated rind of half a lemon
1 tbsp lemon juice
salt and freshly milled black pepper
675g (1½ lb) skinless fish fillets (such as cod, haddock,
**   whiting, halibut, ling, bass or bream), cut into 2.5cm**
**   (1 in) chunks**
2 tbsp chopped fresh parsley

1.   Heat the oil in a large saucepan, add the onions and leeks and cook, stirring occasionally, until softened but not browned.

2.   Stir in the tomatoes and garlic. Add the stock, bay leaf, bouquet garni, lemon rind and lemon juice. Season lightly with salt and pepper.

3.   Bring just to the boil and transfer to the slow cooker. Stir in the fish.

4.   Put the lid on and cook on LOW for 3-6 hours.

5.   Remove the bay leaf and bouquet garni.

6.   Serve sprinkled with parsley.

Soupe Provençale

This soup is based on one served to me by friends during one of my trips to Provence.

Serves 4-6   *Overnight soaking, plus LOW 8-10 hours*

115g (4 oz) dried haricot beans
2 tbsp olive oil
2 medium onions, finely chopped
2 medium carrots, thinly sliced
1 large potato, finely diced
2 garlic cloves, crushed
1 litre (1¾ pints) chicken stock
2 tbsp tomato purée
salt and freshly milled pepper
115g (4 oz) French or runner beans, thinly sliced
handful of fresh basil leaves
freshly grated Parmesan cheese

1. Pour sufficient boiling water over the haricot beans to cover them completely and leave to soak overnight.

2. The next day, preheat the slow cooker on HIGH. Drain the haricot beans.

3. Heat the oil in a large saucepan, add the onions, carrots and potato and cook, stirring occasionally, until softened but not browned.

4. Add the garlic, drained beans, stock, tomato purée, and a little seasoning. Bring to the boil and simmer gently for 5 minutes.

5. Transfer to the slow cooker and stir in the French beans.

6. Put the lid on and cook on LOW for 8-10 hours.

7. Just before serving, adjust seasoning to taste. Roughly tear the basil leaves and stir in.

8. Serve sprinkled with Parmesan cheese.

Split Pea Soup

This is one of my favourite warming winter soups. Serve it with thick slices of warm crusty bread.

Serves 4-6   *Overnight soaking, plus LOW 8-10 hours*

225g (8 oz) dried split peas
115g (4 oz) smoked streaky bacon rashers, finely chopped
1 medium onion, finely chopped
3 celery sticks, thinly sliced
1 litre (1¾ pints) chicken stock
1 tbsp cornflour
½ tsp dried sage
salt and freshly milled black pepper

1. Pour sufficient boiling water over the peas to cover them completely and leave to soak overnight.

2. The next day, preheat the slow cooker on HIGH. Drain the peas.

3. In a large non-stick saucepan, gently cook the bacon, stirring occasionally, until the fat begins to run.

4. Add the onion and celery and cook, stirring occasionally until softened but not browned.

5. Add the drained peas and stock.

6. Blend the cornflour with sufficient cold water to make a smooth pouring cream. Add to the saucepan and bring to the boil, stirring continuously.

7. Add the sage and a little seasoning. Transfer to the slow cooker.

8. Put the lid on and cook on LOW for 8-10 hours.

9. Adjust seasoning to taste before serving.

Cream of Onion Soup

This makes a lovely start to a meal. As well as chopped fresh chives I like to serve it topped with crisp-fried breadcrumbs and a sprinkling of freshly grated Parmesan cheese.

Serves 4-6   *LOW 6-10 hours*

40g (1½ oz) butter
450g (1 lb) onions, finely chopped
55g (2 oz) plain flour
1 litre (1¾ pints) chicken stock
salt and white pepper
150ml (¼ pint) double cream
chopped fresh chives, to serve

1. Heat the butter in a large saucepan, add the onions and cook gently, stirring occasionally, until softened but not browned.

2. Stir in the flour.

3. Remove from the heat and gradually stir in the stock.

4. Season lightly with salt and pepper and bring to the boil. Transfer to the slow cooker.

5. Put the lid on and cook on LOW for 6-10 hours, stirring in the cream for the final 30 minutes.

6. Adjust seasoning to taste and serve sprinkled with chopped chives.

Tomato Soup French Style

Serve with a rustic French loaf or with thick slices of garlic bread.

Serves 4   *LOW 4-8 hours*

4 streaky bacon rashers, finely chopped
1 medium onion, finely chopped
675g (1½ lb) tomatoes, skins and seeds removed,
  roughly chopped
1 garlic clove, crushed
850ml (1½ pints) boiling beef stock (made with just half
  a stock cube)
3 tbsp tomato purée
1 tsp sugar
bay leaf
¼ tsp dried rosemary
salt and freshly milled black pepper

1. In a non-stick frying pan, cook the bacon, stirring occasionally, until the fat begins to run.

2. Add the onion and cook gently, stirring occasionally until softened and just beginning to turn golden brown. Transfer to the slow cooker.

3. Add the remaining ingredients, stirring well.

4. Put the lid on and cook on LOW for 4-8 hours.

5. Remove the bay leaf and adjust seasoning to taste before serving.

Stockpot Soup with Chicken and Sausage

This is a versatile recipe – use vegetables according to season and, in place of frankfurters, use smoked sausages or your favourite butcher's sausages, cooked and sliced.

Serves 4-6   *LOW 8-10 hours*

1 tbsp olive oil
1 medium onion, finely chopped
2 medium carrots, finely diced
1 large potato, finely diced
2 leeks, thinly sliced
2 boneless chicken thighs, skin removed, trimmed and
**   cut into small pieces**
2 tbsp red lentils
2 tbsp tomato purée
1 litre (1¾ pints) beef stock
bay leaf
1 tsp dried oregano
salt and freshly milled black pepper
4 frankfurter sausages, cut into chunks

1. Heat the oil in a large saucepan and add the onion, carrots, potato and leeks. Cook, stirring occasionally, until just beginning to turn golden brown.

2. Add all the remaining ingredients, except the seasoning and frankfurters, and bring to the boil. Transfer to the slow cooker.

3. Put the lid on and cook on LOW for 8-10 hours, removing the bay leaf and adding the frankfurters for the final 30 minutes.

3

MEAT

This chapter includes not only traditional stews and meat puddings, but also special casseroles, such as Veal with Tomatoes and Apricots (page 76), and elegant roasts, such as Spiced Leg of Lamb with Orange (page 72).

Most of the recipes will cook happily all day on LOW. Alternatively, they can be cooked on HIGH ready for serving at lunchtime. You will discover that many casserole-type dishes can be left in the slow cooker for an additional hour or so without really spoiling. All they need is a quick stir before serving.

The cooking time will of course depend on the cut of meat used – for all-day cooking, make sure that you choose a cut of meat that needs long slow cooking in order to tenderise it and develop the maximum flavour.

The basic methods for casseroling and braising are described on pages 16-17 and from these you can decide whether to use the Browning Method or the One-step Method. For best results, some recipes (those including liver or minced meat are good examples) should always be prepared using the Browning Method.

Roasts

Slow-cooked 'roasts' are meltingly tender with a lovely flavour – delicious in fact! However, don't expect meat or poultry that is roasted in the slow cooker to be as crisp as the oven-cooked version. The heat in a slow cooker is gentle and moist; in the oven it is hot and dry.

Choose a joint or bird that fits easily in the slow cooker and allows the lid to fit snugly. Trim off any excess fat and brown evenly on all sides in a frying pan first. With a non-stick pan, it is possible to brown without adding fat.

Transfer to the slow cooker, season and put the lid on. No need to add liquid. Joints of pork and steamed meat puddings should always be cooked on HIGH, to ensure thorough heat penetration. Casseroles of cubed meat (including pork) can be cooked on HIGH or LOW as wished.

When cooked, remove the meat to a serving dish and keep warm. Pour the juices from the slow cooker into a jug and allow it to settle for a moment for the fat to rise to the top. Skim or pour off the excess fat. Strain the juices and heat through to make a delicious gravy.

Roasting times vary greatly according to the size and shape of the meat and the proportion of fat and bone. Use the times in the following table as a guide.

GUIDE TO ROASTING TIMES	
Beef, lamb and veal	LOW 4-10 hours
0.9-1.6kg (2-3½ lb)	HIGH 3-6 hours
Beef, lamb and veal	LOW 7-12 hours
1.6kg-2.25kg (3½-5 lb)	HIGH 5-8 hours
Pork	
0.9-1.6kg (2-3½ lb)	HIGH 3-5 hours
Pork	
1.6kg-2.25kg (3½-5 lb)	HIGH 4-6 hours

Portions

Most of recipes in this chapter serve four. If you are cooking for a smaller number, you should reduce the quantities proportionately, always ensuring that onions, celery and root vegetables are immersed in the liquid. In general, small quantities do not cook well in a large slow cooker.

If you decide to increase the quantity of a casserole-type recipe (maybe it reaches almost to the brim of a large slow cooker), it is important to make sure that the heat can penetrate the mass of food. Consequently, using the Browning Method and adding hot stock means you can cook on either the LOW or HIGH setting. However, if you decide to use the One-step Method, it is important that you add hot liquid at the beginning and cook on HIGH throughout.

Beef and Mushroom Casserole

For really large appetites, and if your slow cooker is large enough, you may wish to increase the quantity of potatoes.

If you are preparing this recipe without pre-browning, put the vegetables at the bottom of the slow cooker to make sure they cook through.

Serves 4   *LOW 7-10 hours*

675g (1½ lb) lean stewing beef, cut into cubes
1 tbsp plain flour
2 tbsp oil
2 medium onions, finely chopped
350g (12 oz) carrots, thinly sliced
450g (1 lb) potatoes, thinly sliced
2 celery sticks, thinly sliced
1 tbsp tomato purée
1 litre (1¾ pints) beef stock
115g (4 oz) button mushrooms
salt and freshly milled black pepper
2 tbsp finely chopped fresh parsley

1. Preheat the slow cooker on HIGH. Toss the beef in the flour.

2. Heat 1 tbsp oil in a large saucepan, add the vegetables and cook quickly, stirring occasionally, until lightly browned. Using a slotted spoon, transfer the vegetables to the slow cooker.

3. Add the remaining 1 tbsp oil to the saucepan, add the beef and brown quickly on all sides.

4. To the beef, add the remaining ingredients, except the parsley. Bring to the boil, stirring continuously, and transfer to the slow cooker.

5. Put the lid on and cook on LOW for 7-10 hours.

6. Before serving, stir well and adjust seasoning to taste. Scatter the parsley over the top.

Geordie Stew with Dumplings

Geordie? It contains Newcastle's favourite tipple of course –
to give this hearty stew a rich flavour.

Serves 4   *LOW 7-10 hours, plus HIGH 30-40 minutes*

675g (1½ lb) lean stewing beef, cut into cubes
1 tbsp plain flour
1 tbsp oil
2 medium onions, thinly sliced
300ml (½ pint) Newcastle Brown Ale
2 tsp ready-made mustard
1 tsp sugar
salt and freshly milled black pepper

Dumplings
85g (3 oz) self-raising flour
25g (1 oz) shredded suet
good pinch of dried mixed herbs
pinch of salt
freshly milled pepper
milk

1.   Preheat the slow cooker on HIGH. Toss the beef in the
      flour.

2.   Heat the oil in a frying pan, add the onions and cook,
      stirring occasionally, until just starting to brown.

3.   Add the beef and cook quickly until brown.

4.   Stir in the brown ale, mustard, sugar and seasoning.
      Bring to the boil, stirring continuously and transfer to
      the slow cooker.

5.   Put the lid on and cook on LOW for 7-10 hours.

6.   Meanwhile, make the dumplings. Combine the flour
      suet, herbs, salt and pepper and mix with sufficient milk
      to make a soft dough. Shape the mixture into four balls.

7.   About 40 minutes before serving, switch the slow
      cooker to HIGH. Arrange the dumplings on top of the
      stew, replace the lid and cook for 30-40 minutes.

Sauerbraten

Sauerbraten (pronounced sour-brar-ten) is a German dish that should be prepared at least two days in advance as the flavour improves as it marinates. This recipe was discovered during one of my frequent visits to the country, where it is traditionally served with boiled potatoes or freshly cooked noodles.

Serves 4-6   *2 days marinating, plus LOW 7-10 hours*

Marinade
300ml (½ pint) wine vinegar
1 onion, sliced
1 carrot, sliced
1 celery stick, sliced
bouquet garni
bay leaf
8 peppercorns
2 cloves

1.3kg (3 lb) piece of beef silverside or topside
salt
1 tbsp oil
4 gingernut biscuits, crumbled
2 tbsp cornflour
150ml (¼ pint) double cream

1. Put all the marinade ingredients into a saucepan and add 300ml (½ pint) water. Bring to the boil and simmer gently for 15 minutes. Remove from the heat and cool completely.

2. Place the beef in a deep non-metallic bowl and pour the marinade over. Cover and refrigerate for 2 days, turning the meat once or twice a day.

3. Lift the beef out of the marinade and pat dry with kitchen paper. Sprinkle with salt.

4. Preheat the slow cooker on HIGH.

5. Heat the oil in a frying pan, add the beef and brown quickly on all sides. Transfer to the slow cooker.

6. Strain the marinade and pour 425ml (¾ pint) over the meat. Add the biscuits.

7. Put the lid on and cook on LOW for 7-10 hours.

8. Lift the beef out of its juices and keep warm. Tip the juices into a small saucepan.

9. Blend the cornflour with a little cold water to make a smooth pouring cream and add to the saucepan. Bring to the boil, stirring continuously, until thickened. Reduce the heat to a minimum, add the cream and allow the sauce to heat through.

10. Serve the sauce with the beef.

Braised Beef

Brisket is a boneless joint that has an excellent flavour and is ideal for long slow cooking. The capacity of your slow cooker will dictate the size of brisket and the quantity of vegetables. The amounts given below should fit easily into a 3.5 litre (6 pint) slow cooker. Remember that the root vegetables must be immersed in the stock if they are to cook evenly.

Serves 4-6   *LOW 8-10 hours*

1.3kg (3 lb) brisket of beef, trimmed of excess fat
salt and freshly milled black pepper
2 medium onions, sliced
6 medium carrots, thinly sliced
1 small swede, cut into small cubes
3 medium potatoes, thinly sliced
1 litre (1¾ pints) boiling beef stock
2 tbsp chopped fresh chives

1.   Preheat the slow cooker on HIGH.

2.   Heat a non-stick frying pan, add the beef and brown quickly on all sides (without adding fat).

3.   Season the joint with salt and pepper and transfer to the slow cooker.

4.   Add the vegetables, packing them around the sides of the beef.

5.   Pour the boiling stock over, making sure that the vegetables are immersed – if necessary, adding a little extra.

6.   Put the lid on and cook on LOW for 8-10 hours.

7.   Lift the meat and vegetables out of the juices and keep warm. Tip the juices into a wide pan, bring to the boil and let them bubble until reduced by half (or until they are as concentrated as you like).

Beef in Barbecue Sauce

Freshly cooked rice or pasta goes well with this dish.

Serves 4   *LOW 7-10 hours*

675g (1½ lb) lean stewing beef, cut into cubes
2 tbsp plain flour
1 tbsp oil
1 medium onion, chopped
400g can tomatoes
3 tbsp wine vinegar
1 tbsp Worcestershire sauce
2 tbsp tomato ketchup
½ tsp chilli powder
salt

1. Preheat the slow cooker on HIGH. Toss the meat in the flour.

2. Heat the oil in a large frying pan, add the onion and cook, stirring occasionally, until lightly browned.

3. Add the beef and brown quickly on all sides. Transfer to the slow cooker.

4. In a blender or food processor, purée the remaining ingredients and pour over the beef and onion.

5. Put the lid on and cook on LOW for 7-10 hours.

Beef Cobbler

This recipe is finished off in a hot oven to cook the scone topping.

Serves 4   *LOW 7-10 hours plus 30 minutes in the oven*

675g (1½ lb) lean stewing beef, cut into cubes
2 tbsp plain flour
1 tbsp oil
1 medium onion, finely sliced
1 roasted red pepper (from a jar or can), cut into strips
400g can chopped tomatoes
1 cooked beetroot, cut into cubes
1 tbsp paprika
salt and freshly milled black pepper
150ml (¼ pint) beef stock

Scone topping
225g (8 oz) self-raising flour
pinch of salt
55g (2 oz) butter
milk

1. Preheat the slow cooker on HIGH. Toss the beef in the flour.

2. Heat the oil in a frying pan, add the onion and cook, stirring occasionally, until lightly browned.

3. Add the beef and brown quickly on all sides.

4. Add the red pepper, tomatoes, beetroot, seasoning and stock. Bring to the boil, stirring, and transfer to the slow cooker.

5. Put the lid on and cook on LOW for 7-10 hours.

6. Preheat the oven to 200°C (400°F) or gas 6.

7. Meanwhile, make the scone topping. Mix together the flour and salt, add the butter and rub in until the mixture resembles breadcrumbs. Stir in sufficient milk to make a fairly stiff dough. Roll out on a floured surface to 1cm (½ in) thick and, using a 7.5cm (3 in) round cutter, cut out as many scones as possible.

8.   Arrange the scones overlapping around the edge of the beef (if your slow-cooker pot is not removable, transfer the contents to an ovenproof dish). Put into the hot oven and cook for 30 minutes or until the scones have risen and are golden brown.

Beef in Red Wine

Delicious served with sautéed potatoes or buttered noodles.

Serves 4   *LOW 7-10 hours*

1 tbsp oil
1 medium onion, chopped
675g (1½ lb) lean stewing beef, cut into cubes
12 black olives
1 garlic clove, crushed
4 large ripe tomatoes, skins and seeds removed,
   roughly chopped
115g (4 oz) button mushrooms
300ml (½ pint) dry red wine
1 tsp dried thyme
salt and freshly milled black pepper
chopped fresh parsley

1.   Preheat the slow cooker on HIGH.

2.   Meanwhile, heat the oil in a large frying pan, add the onion and cook, stirring occasionally, until lightly browned.

3.   Add the beef and brown quickly on all sides. Using a slotted spoon, transfer to the slow cooker.

4.   Add the remaining ingredients, except the parsley.

5.   Put the lid on and cook on LOW for 7-10 hours.

6.   Before serving, remove the bay leaf, stir well and sprinkle with parsley.

Beef Curry

Use mild, medium or hot curry powder, according to your taste. Serve the curry with freshly cooked rice or naan bread, mango chutney and sliced banana.

Serves 4   *LOW 7-10 hours*

2 tbsp plain flour
1 tbsp curry powder
1 tsp ground cumin
1 tsp turmeric
1 tsp ground ginger
salt
675g (1½ lb) lean stewing beef, cut into cubes
1 tbsp oil
1 medium onion, chopped
1 garlic clove, crushed
1 red pepper, seeds removed, sliced
150ml (¼ pint) beef stock
400g can chopped tomatoes
2 tbsp mango chutney
dash of Tabasco sauce
1 tbsp lemon juice
2 cooking apples, peeled, cored, roughly chopped
25g (1 oz) sultanas
25g (1 oz) cashew nuts

1. Preheat the slow cooker on HIGH. Mix together the flour, curry powder, cumin, turmeric, ginger and salt and toss the beef in this mixture.

2. Heat the oil in a large frying pan, add the onion and garlic to the oil and cook gently, stirring occasionally, until softened but not browned.

3. Add the seasoned beef and brown quickly on all sides.

4. Stir in any remaining flour and the remaining ingredients, except the cashew nuts. Bring to the boil, stirring, and transfer to the slow cooker.

5. Put the lid on and cook on LOW for 7-10 hours. Just before serving, stir in the cashew nuts.

Bolognese Sauce

This is good served on freshly cooked pasta, in split jacket potatoes, or in bowls with lots of crusty garlic bread for dipping.

Serves 4   *LOW 5-8 hours*

1 tbsp olive oil
675g (1½ lb) lean minced beef
1 medium onion, finely chopped
2 celery sticks, thinly sliced
1 garlic clove, crushed
400g can chopped tomatoes
1 tbsp plain flour
2 tbsp tomato purée
150ml (¼ pint) beef stock
115g (4 oz) mushrooms, sliced
1 tsp dried mixed herbs
salt and freshly ground black pepper

1.   Preheat the slow cooker on HIGH.

2.   Meanwhile, heat the oil in a saucepan, add the beef and cook, stirring frequently, until lightly browned.

3.   Add the onion, celery and garlic and cook for 2-3 minutes, stirring occasionally.

4.   Blend some of the tomato juice with the flour to make a smooth pouring cream. Stir into the beef with the remaining tomatoes and the tomato purée. Bring to the boil, stirring continuously, until thickened.

5.   Add the remaining ingredients, bring back to the boil and transfer to the slow cooker.

6.   Put the lid on and cook on LOW for 5-8 hours.

7.   Stir well and adjust seasoning to taste before serving.

Italian Pork Chops

Browning the pork chops quickly before slow cooking improves the colour and flavour of the finished dish. Try serving with freshly cooked pasta and a green salad.

Serves 4   *LOW 5-8 hours*

1 medium onion, finely chopped
1 green pepper, seeds removed, diced
1 tbsp olive oil
4 large, thick pork chops (choose lean ones and trim off
  excess fat)
450g (1 lb) courgettes, thinly sliced
6 tomatoes, skins removed, roughly chopped
4 olives stuffed with pimento, sliced
1 tsp dried oregano
1 tbsp wine vinegar
salt and freshly milled black pepper
300ml (½ pint) boiling chicken stock

1. Scatter the onion and pepper in the bottom of the slow cooker.

2. Heat the oil in a non-stick frying pan, add the chops and brown quickly on each side. Transfer to the slow cooker.

3. Stir together the remaining ingredients and spoon over the chops.

4. Put the lid on and cook on LOW for 5-8 hours.

Apple-stuffed Pork Chops

When time allows, I like to brown the chops quickly in a hot frying pan before slow cooking (secure them with string or skewers first).

Serves 4   *LOW 5-8 hours*

25g (1 oz) butter, plus extra for greasing
4 thick pork chops (choose lean ones and trim off
** excess fat)**
salt and freshly milled black pepper
1 medium onion, finely chopped
1 cooking apple, peeled, cored and finely diced
½ tsp dried sage
25g (1 oz) fresh white breadcrumbs
2 tbsp apple juice

1.   Grease the base of the slow cooker pot with a little butter.

2.   Using a sharp knife, slit each chop from the outside edge to the bone to make a pocket. Season lightly inside and out.

3.   Heat the butter in a small saucepan, add the onion and apple and cook gently, stirring occasionally, until softened but not browned. Remove from the heat, add the sage, breadcrumbs and a little salt and pepper. Mix well.

4.   Spoon the stuffing into the chops and arrange them in the slow cooker. Add the apple juice.

5.   Put the lid on and cook on LOW for 5-8 hours.

Devilled Spare Ribs

Use the Chinese-style spare ribs and not spare-rib chops. I have been known to leave these in the slow cooker for up to 10 hours, after which the meat tends to fall off the bone but rarely dries up. Serve them just as they are and follow with a mixed salad tossed in oil-and-vinegar dressing.

Serves 4   *LOW 5-8 hours*

**1kg (2 lb 4 oz) lean pork spare ribs, in one or two racks
    if possible
2 garlic cloves, crushed
1 tsp mustard powder
1 tsp curry powder
1 tsp ground ginger
dash of Tabasco sauce
2 tbsp Worcestershire sauce
2 tbsp tomato purée
salt**

1. Using a sharp knife, cut between the bones, leaving a strip of meat attached to either side of each bone.

2. Mix together the remaining ingredients and brush the sauce over the spare ribs.

3. Arrange in a fairly even layer in the slow cooker.

4. Put the lid on and cook on LOW for 5-8 hours.

Pork and Peas

Knuckle of pork is extremely tasty and there is lots of meat to be found on it. Get one from your local butcher. I usually serve this simply with hot crusty bread.

Serves 4   *Overnight soaking plus HIGH 6-9 hours*

175g (6 oz) dried peas
675g (1½ lb) knuckle of pork (choose a lean one and
  trim off excess fat)
1 medium onion, finely chopped
600ml (1 pint) chicken stock
salt and freshly milled black pepper
1 tbsp cornflour

1. Pour sufficient boiling water over the peas to cover them and leave to soak overnight.

2. Preheat the slow cooker on HIGH.

3. Put the pork into the slow cooker with the onion.

4. Drain the peas, put into a saucepan with the stock and fast boil for 15 minutes.

5. Pour the peas and their liquid over the pork, making sure that the peas are immersed.

6. Put the lid on and cook on HIGH for 6-9 hours.

7. Lift the pork out of the slow cooker and remove the meat from the bone, cutting it into bite-size pieces.

8. Return the meat to the slow cooker and season to taste with salt and pepper.

9. Blend the cornflour with a little cold water to make a smooth pouring cream. Add to the slow cooker, stirring until the sauce thickens.

Creamy Pork with Mushrooms

Serve with rice, pasta or couscous and maybe a side salad of thinly sliced tomatoes and red onion. This recipe is not suitable for freezing.

Serves 4   *LOW 6-8 hours*

1 medium onion, finely chopped
2 celery sticks, thinly sliced
675g (1½ lb) lean stewing pork, cut into cubes
2 tbsp plain flour
salt and freshly milled black pepper
115g (4 oz) mushrooms, sliced
300ml (½ pint) boiling chicken stock
1 egg yolk, beaten
4 tbsp double cream
chopped fresh herbs, such as parsley, coriander or chives

1. Put the onion and celery in the slow cooker.

2. Toss the pork in the flour and add to the slow cooker. Add the seasoning, mushrooms and boiling stock.

3. Put the lid on and cook on LOW for 6-8 hours.

4. Blend the egg yolk with the cream. Just before serving, stir 3 tbsp of the hot sauce into this mixture. Add it to the slow cooker and stir well until the sauce has thickened.

5. Serve immediately sprinkled with herbs.

Lamb Hot Pot

You will probably need to buy tasty lamb pieces such as middle neck from your local butcher. Serve with mashed potatoes or crusty bread to mop up the juices.

Serves 4   *LOW 7-10 hours*

**1kg (2 lb 4 oz) lean pieces of stewing lamb on the bone,
  such as middle neck**
2 tbsp plain flour
1 tbsp olive oil
1 medium onion, finely chopped
2 medium carrots, thinly sliced
salt and freshly milled black pepper
2 tsp horseradish sauce
400g can tomatoes
150ml (¼ pint) lamb stock
2 tsp finely chopped rosemary leaves

1. Preheat the slow cooker on HIGH. Toss the lamb in the flour.

2. Heat the oil in a large frying pan, add the lamb and brown quickly on all sides. Transfer to the slow cooker.

3. Add the onion and carrots to the frying pan and cook, stirring occasionally, until lightly browned.

4. Add the remaining ingredients, bring to the boil and pour over the lamb in the slow cooker.

5. Put the lid on and cook on LOW for 7-10 hours.

6. Adjust seasoning to taste before serving.

Spiced Leg of Lamb with Orange

Leg of lamb becomes meltingly tender in the slow cooker.

Serves 4-6   *LOW 5-10 hours*

1 tbsp olive oil
1.3kg (3 lb) leg of lamb, trimmed of excess fat
½ tsp ground ginger
finely grated rind and juice of 1 orange
salt and freshly milled black pepper
1 tbsp cornflour

1.   Heat the oil in a large frying pan, add the lamb and brown quickly all over.

2.   Mix together the ginger, orange rind, salt and pepper and sufficient orange juice to make a thick paste. Spread this paste over the meat and transfer to the slow cooker.

3.   Put the lid on and cook on LOW for 5-10 hours. If possible, spoon the juices over the lamb once or twice during the final hour.

4.   Lift the lamb out and keep warm. Strain the juices into a small saucepan.

5.   Blend the cornflour with the remaining orange juice to make a smooth paste and stir into the saucepan. Bring to the boil, stirring continuously, until thickened.

6.   Serve the sauce with the lamb.

Middle Eastern Lamb

Couscous is quick to prepare and makes an ideal accompaniment to this delicious mixture.

Serves 4   *LOW 7-10 hours*

1kg (2 lb 4 oz) lean pieces of stewing lamb on the bone, such as middle neck
1 medium onion, finely chopped
1 tbsp plain flour
1 tsp ground cumin
1 tsp turmeric
salt and freshly milled black pepper
425ml (¾ pint) lamb or chicken stock
55g (2 oz) red lentils
25g (1 oz) raisins
25g (1 oz) dates, chopped
1 tbsp lemon juice

1. In a non-stick frying pan, cook the lamb without additional fat until browned on all sides. Transfer to the slow cooker.

2. Add the onion to the fat in the frying pan and cook, stirring occasionally, until lightly browned.

3. Stir in the flour, cumin, turmeric, salt and pepper.

4. Remove from the heat and gradually add the stock, stirring continuously over a medium heat, until the sauce thickens.

5. Add the remaining ingredients and bring to the boil. Pour over the lamb, making sure that the lentils are immersed in the sauce.

6. Put the lid on and cook on LOW for 7-10 hours.

Irish Stew

A hearty meal for those chilly winter days. Adjust the quantity of potatoes to suit the size of your slow cooker.

Serves 4   *LOW 8-12 hours*

675g (1½ lb) potatoes, thinly sliced
3 carrots, thinly sliced
2 onions, finely chopped
1kg (2 lb 4 oz) lean pieces of stewing lamb on the bone, such as middle neck
salt and freshly milled black pepper
boiling lamb or chicken stock

1. Lay the potatoes on the bottom of the slow cooker and cover with the carrots and onions.

2. Arrange the lamb on top of the vegetables. Season with salt and pepper and pour over sufficient boiling stock to cover the lamb.

3. Put the lid on and cook on LOW for 8-12 hours.

Mint-stuffed Breast of Lamb

If time allows, why not brown the rolls of lamb quickly in a little olive oil before putting in the slow cooker.

Serves 4   *LOW 6-10 hours*

115g (4 oz) fresh breadcrumbs
2 tbsp chopped fresh mint
salt and freshly milled black pepper
4 tbsp clear honey
2 breasts of lamb, boned, skinned and trimmed of all excess fat

1. Mix together the first four ingredients.

2. Spread the stuffing evenly over the lamb and roll up each piece from the narrow end. Tie securely with string and cut each roll in half.

3. Place the lamb in the slow cooker, put the lid on and cook on LOW for 6-10 hours.

Moussaka

A simple salad is the only addition required to this tasty Greek dish.

Serves 4   *LOW 6-9 hours*

25g (1 oz) butter, plus extra for greasing
2 medium aubergines, thinly sliced
salt and freshly milled black pepper
2 tsp olive oil
450g (1 lb) lean minced lamb or beef
1 medium onion, finely chopped
1 garlic clove, crushed
¼ tsp ground nutmeg
½ tsp dried oregano
150ml (¼ pint) lamb or beef stock
2 tbsp tomato purée
55g (2 oz) cornflour
600ml (1 pint) milk
grated Parmesan or mature Cheddar cheese

1. Butter the inside of the slow cooker. Arrange the aubergines over the base, seasoning each layer lightly with salt and pepper.

2. Heat the oil in a frying pan, add the mince and cook, stirring occasionally, until starting to brown. Add the onion and garlic and cook for 1-2 minutes, stirring. Season lightly and add the nutmeg, oregano, stock and tomato purée. Bring to the boil and spoon over the aubergines.

3. In a small saucepan, melt the 25g (1 oz) butter, stir in the cornflour and cook gently, stirring, until creamy. Remove from the heat and gradually add the milk, stirring well to prevent lumps forming. Season and return to the heat. Bring to the boil, stirring continuously, until thickened. Pour over the lamb.

4. Put the lid on and cook on LOW for 6-9 hours.

5. If the pot is removable, sprinkle the moussaka with grated cheese and brown under a hot grill.

Veal with Tomatoes and Apricots

Serve with freshly cooked rice or couscous.

Serves 4   *LOW 7-9 hours*

675g (1½ lb) lean stewing veal, cut into strips
2 tbsp plain flour
400g can chopped tomatoes
150ml (¼ pint) boiling veal or chicken stock
1 tbsp wine vinegar
55g (2 oz) dried apricots, halved
1 tsp brown sugar
½ tsp dried mixed herbs
salt and freshly milled pepper

1. Toss the veal in the flour and place in the slow cooker.
   Add the remaining ingredients and stir well.

2. Put the lid on and cook on LOW for 7-9 hours.

Veal Marengo

Good with mashed potatoes, parsnips, squash or celeriac.

Serves 4   *LOW 7-9 hours*

1 medium onion, finely chopped
675g (1½ lb) lean stewing veal, cut into cubes
2 tbsp plain flour
4 tomatoes, skins removed and quartered
115g (4 oz) button mushrooms, sliced
2 tbsp tomato purée
1 garlic clove, crushed
salt and freshly milled pepper
good pinch of dried thyme
150ml (¼ pint) dry white wine
150ml (¼ pint) boiling chicken stock
3 tbsp sherry

1. Scatter the onion in the slow cooker. Toss the veal in
   the flour and put into the slow cooker with the remaining ingredients, except the sherry. Stir well.

2. Put the lid on and cook on LOW for 7-9 hours, stirring in
   the sherry 30 minutes before serving.

Bacon and Leek Pudding

This tasty old-fashioned pudding is made with suet crust pastry and needs to be cooked on HIGH throughout. Serve it with green vegetables or salad.

Serves 4-6   *HIGH 6-8 hours*

175g (6 oz) self-raising flour
85g (3 oz) shredded suet
pinch of salt
freshly milled black pepper
675g (1½ lb) lean unsmoked bacon (preferably in one piece), cut into cubes
1 leek, thinly sliced
2 tbsp chopped fresh parsley

1. Preheat the slow cooker on HIGH. Grease a 1 litre (1¾ pint) pudding basin.

2. Mix together the flour, suet, seasoning and sufficient water to make a soft dough. Reserve one-third for the lid and roll out the remainder on a lightly floured surface and use to line the pudding basin.

3. Put the bacon in a saucepan, cover with cold water, bring slowly to the boil, and then drain and discard the water.

4. Mix the bacon with the leek, parsley and some pepper and pack carefully into the pastry-lined basin. Add 2 tbsp water. (The pudding should not quite fill the basin – to allow space for the crust to rise.)

5. Roll out the remaining pastry to form the lid. Moisten the edges of the pudding with water and press the lid into position.

6. Cover with greased greaseproof paper or foil and lower into the slow cooker using a lifting strap (see page 25). Pour in sufficient boiling water to come half way up the side of the basin.

7. Put the lid on and cook on HIGH for 6-8 hours.

Steak and Kidney Pudding

A family favourite that is really convenient to make with a slow cooker. Cook it on HIGH throughout.

Serves 4-6   *HIGH 6-8 hours*

175g (6 oz) self-raising flour
85g (3 oz) shredded suet
pinch of salt
450g (1 lb) lean stewing steak, cut into cubes
**225g (8 oz) ox or lamb kidney, trimmed and cut into
   cubes**
1 medium onion, finely chopped
freshly milled black pepper

1. Preheat the slow cooker on HIGH. Grease a 1 litre (1¾ pint) pudding basin.

2. Mix together the flour, suet, seasoning and sufficient water to make a soft dough. Reserve one-third for the lid and roll out the remainder on a lightly floured surface and use to line the pudding basin.

3. Mix together the steak, kidney, onion, salt and pepper and pack carefully into the pastry-lined basin. Add 2 tbsp water. (The pudding should not quite fill the basin – to allow space for the crust to rise.)

4. Roll out the remaining pastry to form the lid. Moisten the edges of the pudding with water and press the lid into position.

5. Cover with greased greaseproof paper or foil and lower into the slow cooker using a lifting strap (see page 25). Pour in sufficient boiling water to come half way up the side of the basin.

6. Put the lid on and cook on HIGH for 6-8 hours.

Kidneys Seville

Serve with freshly cooked rice or warm crusty bread.

Serves 4   *LOW 4-8 hours*

15g (½ oz) butter
1 tbsp olive oil
1 medium onion, finely chopped
2 medium carrots, finely diced
115g (4 oz) mushrooms, sliced
3-4 lambs' kidneys per person, skinned, cores removed,
   halved
300ml (½ pint) lamb or chicken stock
3 tbsp orange marmalade
salt and freshly milled black pepper
good pinch of dried thyme
1 tbsp cornflour

1. Heat the butter and oil in a large frying pan, add the onion and carrots and cook, stirring occasionally, until lightly browned.

2. Add the mushrooms. Using a slotted spoon, transfer the vegetables to the slow cooker.

3. Add the kidneys to the fat remaining in the frying pan and cook quickly, stirring occasionally, until browned.

4. Add the stock, marmalade, seasoning and thyme to the kidneys.

5. Blend the cornflour with a little water to make a smooth pouring cream and add into the pan. Bring to the boil, stirring continuously, until thickened. Transfer to the slow cooker.

6. Put the lid on and cook on LOW for 4-8 hours.

7. Stir before serving.

Liver and Bacon

Buy lamb, pig or ox liver – whichever you prefer.

Serves 4   *LOW 4-8 hours*

1 tbsp olive oil
4 lean bacon rashers, chopped
2 medium onions, thinly sliced
450g (1 lb) liver, sliced into four portions
2 tbsp plain flour
salt and freshly milled black pepper
1 tbsp tomato ketchup
425ml (¾ pint) beef stock
1 tsp Worcestershire sauce

1.   Heat the oil in a large frying pan, add the bacon and onions and cook, stirring occasionally, until golden brown. Using a slotted spoon, transfer to the slow cooker.

2.   Toss the liver in the flour, add to the remaining fat in the hot frying pan and brown quickly on both sides.

3.   Season and add the tomato ketchup, stock and Worcestershire sauce. Bring just to the boil, stirring, until thickened. Transfer to the slow cooker.

4.   Put the lid on and cook on LOW for 4-8 hours.

Braised Oxtail

I usually cook this recipe overnight or the day before I want to serve it – giving me time to remove any excess solidified fat.

Serves 4   *LOW 8-12 hours*

8 oxtail pieces, trimmed of excess fat
2 tbsp plain flour
1 tbsp oil
2 medium onions, finely chopped
2 medium carrots, thinly sliced
salt and freshly milled black pepper
150ml (¼ pint) beef stock
400g can chopped tomatoes
1 tsp dried mixed herbs
2 tbsp lemon juice

1. Preheat the slow cooker on HIGH. Toss the oxtail pieces in the flour.

2. Heat the oil in a large saucepan, add the onions and carrots and cook, stirring occasionally, until golden brown. Using a slotted spoon, transfer to the slow cooker.

3. Add the oxtail pieces to the pan and brown quickly on all sides.

4. Add the remaining ingredients to the oxtail, except the lemon juice. Bring to the boil, stirring continuously, until thickened. Transfer to the slow cooker.

5. Put the lid on and cook on LOW for 8-12 hours.

6. Transfer to a clean container and cool quickly. Remove the solidified fat from the surface before adding the lemon juice and heating through in a pan.

Lamb and Bean Cassoulet

This is a large cassoulet! You may need to adjust the quantities, depending on the size of your slow cooker. Hot garlic bread is my favourite accompaniment here.

Serves 6   *Overnight soaking plus LOW 8-12 hours*

450g (1 lb) dried haricot beans
450g (1 lb) lean unsmoked streaky bacon, cut into small pieces
2 tbsp olive oil
450g (1 lb) lean lamb, cut into cubes
2 medium onions, thinly sliced
2 garlic cloves, crushed
4 tbsp tomato purée
1 tsp dried oregano
1 tsp dried thyme
300ml (½ pint) dry white wine
300ml (½ pint) chicken or beef stock
225g (8 oz) garlic sausage, cut into cubes
salt and freshly milled black pepper

1. Pour sufficient boiling water over the beans to cover them and leave to soak overnight.

2. Preheat the slow cooker on HIGH.

3. Drain the beans and put into a large saucepan. Cover with 1 litre (1¾ pints) fresh water and fast boil for 10 minutes. Add the bacon and boil for a further 5 minutes. Skim the surface to remove any scum, then using a slotted spoon, transfer the bacon and beans to the slow cooker. Reserve the cooking liquor.

4. Heat the oil in a frying pan, add the lamb and brown quickly on all sides. Using a slotted spoon, transfer the lamb to the slow cooker.

5. Add the onions to the remaining fat and cook, stirring occasionally, until softened but not browned. Transfer to the slow cooker and stir in the garlic, tomato purée and herbs.

6. Put the wine and stock into the frying pan and bring just to the boil. Pour over the contents of the slow cooker.

7. Heat the reserved cooking liquor and add sufficient to ensure that the ingredients are totally immersed.

8. Put the lid on and cook on LOW for 8-12 hours, adding the garlic sausage and seasoning for the final 30 minutes.

Sausage and Onion Casserole

Use your favourite good-quality sausages. This dish is particularly good served with mashed potatoes.

Serves 4   *LOW 5-8 hours*

1 tbsp oil
4-8 sausages
2 medium onions, finely chopped
2 tbsp plain flour
300ml (½ pint) chicken or beef stock
2 tbsp chutney
1 tbsp Worcestershire sauce
salt and freshly milled black pepper

1. Preheat the slow cooker on HIGH.

2. Meanwhile, heat the oil in a frying pan, add the sausages and quickly brown on all sides. Transfer to the slow cooker.

3. Add the onions to the pan and cook, stirring occasionally, until softened but not browned.

4. Stir the flour into the onions and cook gently, stirring for 1-2 minutes.

5. Remove from the heat and gradually stir in the stock. Bring to the boil, stirring continuously, until thickened.

6. Stir in the chutney, Worcestershire sauce and seasoning. Pour over the sausages in the slow cooker.

7. Put the lid on and cook on LOW for 5-8 hours.

4

POULTRY AND GAME

The guidelines given at the beginning of Chapter 3 also broadly apply to poultry and game. In addition, please remember that *whole* birds are best cooked on HIGH only – to ensure thorough cooking. *Portions* can be cooked on HIGH or LOW as you wish. Before serving, always make sure that the poultry or game is cooked throughout – juices should run clear when the thickest part is pierced with a skewer or sharp knife.

GUIDE TO ROASTING TIMES	
Chicken 1.3kg (3 lb)	HIGH 3-4 hours
Duck 1.8kg (4 lb)	HIGH 5-6 hours
Pheasant Large	HIGH 3-4 hours

Chicken and Mushroom Casserole

Use chicken pieces with or without skin – the choice is yours.

Serves 4   *LOW 4-6 hours*

8 chicken thighs, on the bone
1 tbsp plain flour
25g (1 oz) butter
1 medium onion, finely chopped
2 celery sticks, thinly sliced
225g (8 oz) mushrooms, thinly sliced
1 garlic clove, crushed
300ml (½ pint) chicken stock
salt and freshly milled pepper
3 tbsp soured cream
chopped fresh parsley

1. Preheat the slow cooker on HIGH. Toss the chicken in the flour.

2. Heat the butter in a frying pan, add the chicken and cook quickly until golden brown on all sides. Transfer to the slow cooker.

3. Add the onion and celery to the remaining butter in the pan and cook, stirring occasionally, until softened but not browned.

4. Add the mushrooms and garlic to the pan and stir in the stock. Bring to the boil, season and pour over the chicken, making sure the vegetables are immersed (though it doesn't matter if the chicken isn't completely covered by the sauce).

5. Put the lid on and cook on LOW for 4-6 hours.

6. About 10 minutes before serving, stir in the cream and sprinkle with parsley.

Chicken in Apple Juice with Sweetcorn

Good served with new or baby potatoes and a green vegetable such as broccoli.

Serves 4   LOW 5-8 hours including 30 minutes on HIGH

1 medium onion, finely chopped
3 celery sticks, thinly sliced
1 green pepper, seeds removed, diced
4 chicken quarters, skin removed
salt and freshly milled pepper
1 tsp dried tarragon
300ml (½ pint) apple juice
1 tbsp cornflour
198g can of sweetcorn

1. Put the onion, celery and green pepper into the slow cooker.

2. Add the chicken, seasoning and tarragon and pour the apple juice over.

3. Put the lid on and cook on LOW for 5-8 hours.

4. About 30 minutes before serving, switch to HIGH. Blend the cornflour with the liquid from the can of sweetcorn to make a smooth paste and stir into the slow cooker with the sweetcorn. Continue cooking on HIGH for the final 30 minutes.

Sweet and Sour Chicken

Freshly cooked rice goes well with this tangy dish.

Serves 4   *LOW 4-6 hours*

1 tbsp oil
8 chicken thighs, skin removed
1 medium onion, finely chopped
1 green pepper, seeds removed, diced
1 celery stick, thinly sliced
2 tbsp cornflour
227g can pineapple slices or chunks in natural juice,
**   drained and chopped and juice reserved**
4 tbsp wine vinegar
1 tbsp soy sauce
85g (3 oz) brown sugar
salt and freshly milled pepper

1. Preheat the slow cooker on HIGH.

2. Heat the oil in a large frying pan, add the chicken and
    cook quickly, turning frequently, until evenly browned.
    Using a slotted spoon, transfer to the slow cooker.

3. To the remaining oil in the pan, add the onion, green
    pepper and celery and cook, stirring occasionally, until
    softened but not browned.

4. Blend the cornflour with the pineapple juice and top up
    with sufficient water to make 300ml (½ pint). Add to the
    pan with the vinegar, soy sauce, pineapple, sugar and
    seasoning.

5. Bring to the boil, stirring continuously, until thickened
    and pour over the chicken.

6. Put the lid on and cook on LOW for 4-6 hours.

Chicken in White Wine Sauce

Serve with freshly cooked noodles and a crisp green salad. This recipe is not suitable for freezing.

Serves 4   *LOW 3-5 hours*

4 chicken breast joints, skin removed
25g (1 oz) butter
1 medium onion, finely chopped
115g (4 oz) mushrooms, sliced
1 tbsp cornflour
425ml (¾ pint) dry white wine
1 tsp dried thyme
salt and freshly milled pepper
1 egg yolk
4 tbsp double cream

1. Place the chicken joints in the slow cooker.

2. Heat the butter in a frying pan, add the onion and cook, stirring occasionally, until softened but not browned. Stir in the mushrooms.

3. Blend the cornflour with a little of the wine to make a smooth pouring cream. Pour the remaining wine into the fry pan with the blended cornflour, thyme and seasoning. Bring to the boil, stirring continuously, until thickened. Pour over the chicken.

4. Put the lid on and cook on LOW for 3-5 hours.

5. Just before serving, beat together the egg yolk and cream and stir in a few tablespoons of hot sauce from the slow cooker. Pour this mixture into the slow cooker and stir until the sauce thickens.

Chicken and Orange Curry

Serve with naan bread to mop up the sauce.

Serves 4   *LOW 3-6 hours*

1 tbsp oil
4 chicken thighs and 4 chicken drumsticks
1 medium onion, finely chopped
1 green pepper, seeds removed, diced
1 garlic clove, crushed
1 tbsp curry powder
1 tsp ground cumin
1 apple, peeled, cored and roughly chopped
finely grated rind of 1 orange
300ml (½ pint) unsweetened orange juice
1 chicken stock cube
1 tbsp orange marmalade
25g (1 oz) sultanas
salt
1 tbsp cornflour
fresh orange slices, to garnish

1. Preheat the slow cooker on HIGH.

2. Heat the oil in a large frying pan, add the chicken and brown quickly on all sides. Transfer to the slow cooker.

3. Add the onion, green pepper and garlic to the pan and cook, stirring occasionally, until softened but not browned.

4. Stir in the curry powder and cumin and mix well. Add the remaining ingredients, except the cornflour, and bring to the boil, stirring. Pour over the chicken.

5. Put the lid on and cook on LOW for 3-6 hours.

6. About 30 minutes before serving, switch to HIGH. Blend the cornflour with a little cold water to make a smooth pouring cream and stir into the slow cooker. Replace the lid and leave to thicken.

7. Serve garnished with fresh orange slices.

Chicken Creole

Butter, tomatoes, onion, green pepper and celery are signature ingredients of Creole dishes. Serve this one with freshly cooked rice.

Serves 4   *LOW 3-6 hours*

1 tbsp plain flour
1 tsp paprika
4 chicken thighs
25g (1 oz) butter
1 medium onion, finely chopped
1 green pepper, seeds removed, diced
1 red pepper, seeds removed, diced
1 celery stick, thinly sliced
225g (8 oz) tomatoes, skins and seeds removed,
   roughly chopped
300ml (½ pint) chicken stock
1 tbsp tomato purée
½ tsp Tabasco sauce, or to taste
salt and freshly milled black pepper

1.   Preheat the slow cooker on HIGH.

2.   Mix together the flour and paprika and toss the chicken joints in this.

3.   Heat the butter in a frying pan, add the chicken and cook quickly until evenly browned. Transfer to the slow cooker.

4.   Add the onion and green and red peppers to the pan and cook, stirring occasionally, until softened but not browned.

5.   Stir in the remaining ingredients, bring to the boil and pour over the chicken.

6.   Put the lid on and cook on LOW for 3-6 hours.

Chicken in Red Wine

I like to serve this with new or baby potatoes and a side salad of tomatoes, red onion and black olives.

Serves 4   *LOW 4-6 hours*

25g (1 oz) butter
2 streaky bacon rashers, chopped
1 medium onion, finely chopped
4 chicken joints
115g (4 oz) mushrooms, sliced
2 garlic cloves, crushed
1 tbsp cornflour
150ml (¼ pint) dry red wine
150ml (¼ pint) chicken stock
salt and freshly milled black pepper
chopped fresh parsley

1. Preheat the slow cooker on HIGH.

2. Meanwhile, heat the butter in a frying pan, add the bacon and onion and cook, stirring occasionally, until softened but not browned. Using a slotted spoon, transfer to the slow cooker.

3. Add the chicken to the pan and cook quickly until browned on all sides. Add the mushrooms and garlic.

4. Blend the cornflour with a little wine to make a smooth pouring cream. Add the wine, stock and the blended cornflour to the chicken. Bring to the boil over a medium heat, stirring, until thickened. Add seasoning and transfer to the slow cooker.

5. Put the lid on and cook on LOW for 4-6 hours.

6. Serve garnished with parsley.

Slow Cooked Chicken with Tarragon

Make sure the chicken will fit comfortably into your slow cooker. Dried tarragon works better than fresh in this recipe.

Serves 4-6   *HIGH 3-4 hours*

15g (½ oz) butter
1 tbsp olive oil
1.3kg (3 lb) oven-ready chicken
salt and freshly milled black pepper
finely grated rind of 1 lemon
1 tsp dried tarragon
juice of ½ lemon
1 tbsp cornflour

1. Heat the butter and oil in a large frying pan, add the chicken and cook quickly, turning frequently, until browned all over. Transfer to the slow cooker.

2. Lightly season the chicken with salt and pepper. Sprinkle the lemon rind, tarragon and lemon juice over.

3. Put the lid on and cook on HIGH for 3-4 hours.

4. Lift the cooked chicken out of the slow cooker and keep warm.

5. Strain the juices into a jug, allow them to settle for a moment, then pour or spoon off the fat floating on top. Pour the remaining juices into a small pan.

6. Blend the cornflour with a little cold water to make a smooth paste and add to the juices with sufficient water to make the required amount of gravy. Bring to the boil, stirring, until thickened. Adjust the seasoning to taste and serve with the chicken.

Chicken Risotto

A good way to use chicken left over from a roast. Don't be tempted to use real risotto rice – it is too starchy and you will end up with a sticky mass. Use easy-cook rice.

Serves 4   *LOW 2-3 hours*

1 tbsp oil
1 medium onion, finely chopped
2 celery sticks, thinly sliced
225g (8 oz) cooked chicken, cut into small pieces
175g (6 oz) easy-cook long grain rice
1 roasted red pepper (from a jar or can), chopped
198g can sweetcorn, drained
425g (¾ pint) chicken stock
salt and freshly milled black pepper
1 tsp dried mixed herbs

1.　Heat the oil in a large frying pan, add the onion and celery and cook, stirring occasionally, until softened but not browned.

2.　Stir in the chicken and rice and cook over a low heat, stirring, for a couple of minutes.

3.　Add the remaining ingredients, bring just to the boil and transfer to the slow cooker.

4.　Put the lid on and cook on LOW for 2-3 hours. If convenient, it helps to stir the risotto once or twice during the final hour of cooking.

Chicken and Ham Pudding

Cook this savoury pudding on HIGH throughout. Serve it with a large mixed salad.

Serves 4   *HIGH 4-7 hours*

Suet pastry
225g (8 oz) self-raising flour
115g (4 oz) shredded suet
pinch of salt

Filling
4 boneless chicken thighs, skin removed
salt and freshly milled pepper
4 cooked ham slices
1 medium onion, finely chopped
55g (2 oz) mushrooms, finely chopped
½ tsp dried tarragon

1. Preheat the slow cooker on HIGH. Grease a 1 litre (1¾ pint) pudding basin.

2. Mix together the flour, suet, seasoning and sufficient water to make a soft dough. Reserve one-third for the lid and roll out the remainder on a lightly floured surface and use to line the pudding basin.

3. Season each chicken thigh and wrap in a slice of ham. Arrange the four parcels in the pastry-lined basin.

4. Mix together the onion, mushrooms and tarragon with a little seasoning and scatter over the chicken. Add 3 tbsp water.

5. Roll out the remaining pastry to form the lid. Moisten the edges of the pudding with water and press the lid into position.

6. Cover with greased greaseproof paper or foil and lower into the slow cooker using a lifting strap (see page 25). Pour in sufficient boiling water to come half way up the side of the basin. Put the lid on and cook on HIGH for 4-7 hours.

Duck with Orange Sauce

Depending on the size of your slow cooker, the duck may be oooked whole or cut Into four portions. A whole bird must be cooked on HIGH throughout. Joints can be cooked on LOW.

Serves 4

Whole: HIGH 5-6 hours
Portions: LOW 4-8 hours

1.8kg (4 lb) duck
salt and freshly milled black pepper
25g (1 oz) butter
1 onion, finely chopped
2 tbsp orange marmalade
1 tbsp cornflour
juice of 1 orange
300ml (½ pint) chicken stock
finely grated rind of 1 orange
3 tbsp orange liqueur

1. Prick the skin of the duck all over. Heat a large non-stick frying pan and brown the duck quickly on all sides. Transfer to the slow cooker and sprinkle with salt and pepper.

2. Put the lid on and cook for the recommended time (see above).

3. Meanwhile, heat the butter in a medium saucepan, add the onion and cook, stirring occasionally, until lightly browned. Stir in the marmalade. Blend the cornflour with the orange juice to make a smooth pouring cream and add to the pan with the stock and orange rind. Bring to the boil, stirring, until thickened.

4. Lift the duck from the slow cooker and pour the juices into a jug and leave to settle. Return the duck to the slow cooker. (If wished, the duck may be portioned at this stage for easier serving.) Pour away the fat on top of the juices and strain into the sauce. Stir well, season to taste and pour over the duck.

5. Replace the lid and switch the slow cooker to LOW until you are ready to serve, stirring in the orange liqueur just before serving.

Pigeons in Cranberry Sauce

Make sure that four pigeons will fit into your slow cooker.

Serves 4   *LOW 6-10 hours*

25g (1 oz) butter
2 streaky bacon rashers, finely chopped
4 oven-ready pigeons
1 medium onion, finely chopped
1 medium carrot, thinly sliced
1 celery stick, thinly sliced
300ml (½ pint) chicken stock
1 tbsp cornflour
3 tbsp cranberry sauce
salt and freshly milled black pepper

1. Heat the butter in a large frying pan, add the bacon and cook, stirring occasionally, until lightly browned.

2. Add the pigeons and brown quickly on all sides.

3. Using a slotted spoon, transfer the pigeons and bacon to the slow cooker.

4. To the remaining fat, add the onion, carrot and celery and cook, stirring occasionally, until golden brown. Add the stock.

5. Blend the cornflour with a little cold water to make a smooth pouring cream and add to the pan. Bring to the boil, stirring continuously, until thickened. Stir in the cranberry sauce and seasoning. Pour over the pigeons.

6. Put the lid on and cook on LOW for 6-10 hours.

Fricassée of Turkey

You may like to replace half the chicken stock with dry white wine. Rice is the usual accompaniment but I like it with roasted vegetables.

Serves 4   *LOW 3½-6 hours*
                              plus HIGH 30 minutes

675g (1½ lb) turkey meat, cut into cubes
25g (1 oz) butter
1 medium onion, finely chopped
115g (4 oz) mushrooms, sliced
bouquet garni
sliver of lemon zest
salt and freshly milled pepper
300ml (½ pint) chicken stock
2 tbsp cornflour
4 tbsp milk

1. Put the turkey into the slow cooker.

2. Heat the butter in a frying pan, add the onion and cook, stirring occasionally, until softened but not browned.

3. Stir in the remaining ingredients, except the cornflour and milk, bring to the boil and pour over the turkey.

4. Put the lid on and cook on LOW for 3½-6 hours.

5. About 30 minutes before serving, remove the bouquet garni and lemon zest and switch to HIGH. Blend the cornflour with the milk to make a smooth pouring cream. Stir into the slow cooker. Replace the lid and leave to thicken for the final 30 minutes.

Grouse in Port Wine

You will need a large slow cooker for this recipe. The cooking time will depend on the age of the birds.

Serves 4

Overnight marinating plus

young grouse: LOW 4-7 hours

mature grouse: LOW 6-10 hours

1 medium onion, finely chopped
1 medium carrot, finely diced
1 celery stick, thinly sliced
bouquet garni
150ml (¼ pint) port
4 oven-ready grouse
25g (1 oz) butter
2 tbsp tomato purée
salt and freshly milled black pepper
2 tbsp redcurrant jelly

1. Put the onion, carrot, celery and bouquet garni into a small saucepan with 300ml (½ pint) water. Bring to the boil, cover and simmer for 15 minutes. Remove from the heat and cool. Pour into a deep, non-metallic container. Stir in the port and add the grouse. Cover and leave to marinate overnight in the refrigerator. (Turn the grouse over once or twice during marinating if possible.)

2. The next day, remove the grouse from the marinade and pat dry with kitchen paper.

3. Heat the butter in a frying pan, add the grouse and brown quickly on all sides. Transfer to the slow cooker.

4. Stir the tomato purée into the marinade and season lightly. Pour over the grouse.

5. Put the lid on and cook for the recommended time (see above).

6. Remove the grouse and keep warm. Discard the bouquet garni. Liquidise or process the sauce and transfer to a small pan. Add the redcurrant jelly and heat through, stirring well. Serve with the grouse.

Braised Pheasant

The moist heat of the slow cooker is ideal for game birds like pheasant.

Serves 4   *HIGH 3-4 hours*

55g (2 oz) butter
2 lean bacon rashers, finely chopped
1 medium onion, finely chopped
2 celery sticks, thinly sliced
115g (4 oz) mushrooms, thinly sliced
1 large oven-ready pheasant or 2 small ones
salt and freshly milled black pepper
½ tsp thyme
2 tbsp tomato purée
¼ tsp grated nutmeg
150ml (¼ pint) chicken stock or water
150ml (¼ pint) medium sherry
1 tbsp cornflour
bay leaf

1. Heat half the butter in a large frying pan, add the bacon, onion and celery and cook, stirring occasionally, until lightly browned. Stir in the mushrooms. Using a slotted spoon, transfer to the slow cooker.

2. Season the pheasant lightly. Heat the remaining butter in the frying pan, add the pheasant(s) and brown quickly on all sides. Transfer to the slow cooker and sprinkle with the thyme.

3. Put the tomato purée and nutmeg into the frying pan, stirring well. Add the stock and sherry. Blend the cornflour with a little cold water to make a smooth pouring cream and add to the pan. Bring to the boil, stirring continuously, until thickened. Season and add the bay leaf. Pour over the pheasant(s).

4. Put the lid on and cook on HIGH for 3-4 hours.

5. Lift out the pheasant(s) and keep warm. Remove the bay leaf. Liquidise or process the sauce and heat through in a small pan. Adjust the seasoning to taste and serve with the pheasant.

Rabbit Casserole with Prunes

The sweetness of the prunes complements the rabbit meat beautifully.

Serves 4   *LOW 6-8 hours*

1kg (2 lb 4 oz) rabbit pieces
2 tbsp plain flour
25g (1 oz) butter
1 medium onion, finely chopped
2 medium carrots, thinly sliced
400g can chopped tomatoes
300ml (½ pint) chicken stock
8 dried prunes
½ tsp dried sage
salt and freshly milled pepper

1. Preheat the slow cooker on HIGH. Toss the rabbit in the flour.

2. Heat the butter in a large frying pan, add the rabbit and quickly brown on all sides. Transfer to the slow cooker.

3. Add the onion and carrots to the pan and cook, stirring occasionally, until lightly browned.

4. Put the remaining ingredients into the pan and bring to the boil, stirring. Transfer to the slow cooker, making sure that the vegetables are immersed in the liquid.

5. Put the lid on and cook on LOW for 6-8 hours.

6. Adjust the seasoning to taste before serving.

5

FISH

In a slow cooker, fish cooks very gently and, unlike with conventional cooking, it does not need timing to the minute. Nevertheless, fish cannot be left in the slow cooker all day or it is likely to dry and toughen. Consequently, cooking times for fish are comparatively shorter than those for meat or vegetables. While it is still possible to gain a few hours away from the kitchen as the fish cooks, equally it is good to be at home knowing that the fish is cooking without the need for constant attention. What's more, the water seal around the rim traps in the smell of cooking fish.

Baking Guidelines
This is ideal for steaks or whole fish such as trout.

1. Grease the inside of the slow cooker and preheat if wished.

2. Wash and dry the fish. Remove the head and tail if necessary so that the fish fits easily into the slow cooker.

3. Put the fish into the slow cooker and dot with butter.

4. Put the lid on. Cook steaks for 2-3 hours on LOW or 1-2 hours on HIGH.

    Cook whole fish for 3-4 hours on LOW or 1-2 hours on HIGH.

Poaching Guidelines
1. Grease the inside of the slow cooker and preheat if wished.

2. Wash and dry the fish. Remove the head and tail, if necessary, so that the fish fits easily into the slow cooker.

3. Place the fish in the slow cooker and sprinkle with seasoning and flavourings such as herbs, finely chopped shallot or onion, or finely grated lemon or orange rind.

4. Pour sufficient liquid over to half cover it – use water, fish stock, water and vinegar, cider, beer, wine or fruit juice. Milk should be added only at the end of cooking to avoid curdling.

5. Put the lid on and cook for 2-3 hours on LOW or 1-2 hours on HIGH.

6. Fish that is to be served cold should be transferred to a dish and allowed to cool in its liquor.

Casseroling Guidelines

1. Grease the inside of the slow cooker and preheat if wished.

2. Wash and dry the fish. Cut into even-size pieces and put into the slow cooker.

3. Heat a little oil or butter in a frying pan, add the vegetables (such as thinly sliced or diced onions, peppers, celery, root vegetables, etc), and cook, stirring occasionally, until they are softened but not browned.

4. Season the vegetables and add herbs and spices if wished.

5. Add about 300ml (½ pint) liquid to the frying pan – use water, fish stock, water and vinegar, cider, beer, wine or fruit juice.

6. To thicken the casserole, blend 1 tablespoonful of cornflour with a little water to make a smooth pouring cream and add to the pan. Bring to the boil, stirring continuously, until thickened. Pour the sauce over the fish.

7. Put the lid on and cook for 2-3 hours on LOW or 1-2 hours on HIGH.

Stuffed Plaice in Celery Sauce

If you decide to reduce the amount of fish, you will still need to use the same quantity of celery soup.

Serves 4   *LOW 2-3½ hours*

2 tsp oil, plus extra for greasing
2 lean bacon rashers, finely chopped
55g (2 oz) button mushrooms, finely chopped
25g (1 oz) fresh white breadcrumbs
salt and freshly milled pepper
4 plaice fillets, skins removed
300g can condensed celery soup

1. Heat the oil in a small pan, add the bacon and cook, stirring occasionally, until golden brown. Remove from the heat and stir in the mushrooms, breadcrumbs and seasoning. Mix well and cool.

2. Grease the inside of the slow cooker.

3. Cut each fillet lengthways to make 8 half-fillets.

4. Spread the bacon mixture over the skinned side of each plaice fillet. Roll each fillet from the narrow end and secure with wooden cocktail sticks. Arrange in the slow cooker.

5. Spoon the soup into the slow cooker, spreading it evenly over the rolls. Don't worry if it looks too thick – it will thin during cooking.

6. Put the lid on and cook on LOW for 2-3½ hours.

7. Carefully lift the fish on to warmed plates or a serving dish and remove the cocktail sticks. Stir the sauce well and spoon over the fish.

Soused Herring

This dish can be served hot or cold. Accompany it with slices of lemon and brown bread and butter. Ask your fishmonger to bone the herrings, remove the tails and fins and cut each fish into two fillets.

Serves 4 as a starter
or 2 as a main course   *LOW 2-4 hours*

4 small herrings, bones removed
salt and freshly milled pepper
150ml (¼ pint) wine vinegar
10 black peppercorns
2 bay leaves
2 strips of lemon zest

1. Rinse the herring fillets and pat dry. Season the cut sides lightly with salt and pepper. Roll up from the tail end and secure with wooden cocktail sticks. Place in the slow cooker.

2. Put the remaining ingredients into a small saucepan. Add 150ml (¼ pint) water and bring to the boil. Pour the mixture over the herrings.

3. Put the lid on and cook on LOW for 2-4 hours.

4. Carefully lift the rolls out of the slow cooker and remove the sticks. Pour the liquid over.

Fish Florentine

Serve with crusty bread and a green salad.

Serves 4   *LOW 2-3 hours*

225g (8 oz) frozen spinach, thawed
4 skinless white fish steaks or fillet steaks, such as cod,
   haddock, hake, whiting
salt and freshly milled pepper
25g (1 oz) butter
1 tbsp cornflour
300m (½ pint) milk
115g (4 oz) cheese such as mature Cheddar, grated
3 tomatoes, sliced

1.   Grease the inside of the slow cooker. Spread the spinach evenly over the base and arrange the cod on top. Season with salt and pepper.

2.   In a small saucepan, melt the butter and stir in the cornflour. Stir over a low heat until bubbling and creamy. Remove from the heat and gradually stir in the milk. Return to the heat and cook, stirring continuously, until thickened. Season with salt and some pepper and stir in three-quarters of the cheese until just melted.

3.   Pour the cheese sauce over the fish and spinach, covering it completely. Arrange the tomato slices around the edge.

4.   Put the lid on and cook on LOW for 2-3 hours.

5.   Sprinkle the remaining cheese on top. If the slow cooker pot is removable, put under a hot grill until golden brown.

Trout with Buttered Almonds

Choose your fish to fit your slow cooker. If you cook more than two whole trout, make sure they can lie side by side in the slow cooker in a single layer.

Serves 2   *LOW 3-4 hours*

2 whole trout, cleaned and heads and tails removed
salt and freshly milled pepper
55g (2 oz) flaked almonds
55g (2 oz) butter
lemon wedges, to serve

1. Grease the inside of the slow cooker with some butter.

2. Rinse the fish and pat dry. Season inside and out with a little salt and pepper.

3. Arrange the trout, head to tail, in the slow cooker. Sprinkle with the almonds and dot with the butter.

4. Put the lid on and cook on LOW for 3-4 hours.

5. Serve with lemon wedges for squeezing over.

Mediterranean Fish Casserole

A French baguette or Italian ciabatta bread goes well with this – to make sure you mop up all the lovely sauce.

Serves 4   *LOW 2-4 hours*

1 tbsp olive oil
1 medium onion, finely chopped
1 green pepper, seeds removed, diced
450g (1 lb) white fish (such as cod, whiting, ling) cut into cubes
115g (4 oz) squid, heads removed and discarded
4 anchovy fillets, chopped
8 green or black olives, sliced
1 garlic clove, crushed
salt and freshly milled black pepper
½ tsp dried thyme or oregano
300ml (½ pint) white wine or fish stock
115g (4 oz) cooked peeled prawns
4 tbsp double or soured cream
1 tbsp chopped fresh parsley

1.   Heat the oil in a saucepan, add the onion and green pepper and cook, stirring occasionally, until softened but not browned. Using a slotted spoon, transfer to the slow cooker.

2.   Add the remaining ingredients to the slow cooker, except the prawns, cream and parsley, and stir together.

3.   Put the lid on and cook on LOW for 2-4 hours, adding the prawns for the final 30 minutes.

4.   Just before serving, gently stir in the cream and sprinkle with the chopped parsley.

Mackerel with Apple

Ask your fishmonger to clean and bone the mackerel.

Serves 4   *LOW 2½-3½ hours*

4 mackerel fillets
salt and freshly milled pepper
15g (½ oz) butter
2 eating apples, peeled, cored and finely chopped
finely grated rind of ½ lemon
juice of ½ lemon

1. Grease the inside of the slow cooker.

2. Rinse the fish and pat dry. Season the cut side of the fillets lightly with salt and pepper.

3. Melt the butter in a small pan, add the apple and lemon rind and cook, stirring frequently, until the apple is softened but not browned. Add 1 tsp of the lemon juice.

4. Spread the apple mixture over the cut side of the mackerel fillets. Roll up from the head end and secure with wooden cocktail sticks.

5. Place the rolls in the slow cooker and sprinkle with the remaining lemon juice.

6. Put the lid on and cook on LOW for 2½-3½ hours.

7. Remove the sticks before serving.

6

VEGETABLES

Whether you want a vegetable dish as a main course, as a starter, or to accompany meat or fish, the slow cooker does it with the minimum of fuss.

It is especially good for vegetables that would easily overcook during normal cooking. Ratatouille, for example, is a luxurious French vegetable stew, which can all too easily become an indescribable mush if not carefully watched – yet in the slow cooker each slice of courgette and aubergine retains its shape and the flavours develop to the full.

Stuffed vegetables that are cooked in the oven, such as peppers and tomatoes, tend to collapse if cooked only a few minutes too long. In a slow cooker they retain their shape for hours.

Root vegetables (like carrots, potatoes, parsnips and celeriac), celery, onions and leeks cook well in the slow cooker too, though they take much longer than you would imagine. Cut them into even-size pieces and they will cook beautifully. When they are mixed in a casserole with meat, it's best to slice them thinly or cut into small dice.

Cooking can be speeded up by quickly cooking these vegetables in oil or butter before being added to the slow cooker. Alternatively, they could be brought to the boil in a pan before being transferred to the slow cooker.

Guidelines for Casseroling Vegetables

1. Peel or prepare the vegetables and cut them into even-size pieces or slices.

2. Put a little oil or butter in a large frying pan or saucepan, add the vegetables and cook, stirring occasionally, until slightly softened. Alternatively, omit the fat and simply put the vegetables in the pan.

3. Sprinkle with seasoning and herbs.

4. Pour over sufficient liquid to barely cover the vegetables. Remember that vegetables produce their own liquids during cooking and you need to take care that you don't end up with too much. Nevertheless the vegetables need to be immersed if they are to cook evenly (and if potatoes are not to discolour).

5. Bring to the boil and transfer to the slow cooker.

6. Put the lid on and cook on LOW for 6-10 hours or on HIGH for 3-5 hours.

Potatoes

If you prefer potatoes to be served whole rather than cut small into a meat stew, it is possible to cook them whole in the slow cooker. The secret is foil. Wrap each potato in foil and place on top of the food in the casserole. The foil will concentrate the heat and the potatoes should cook through in the 6-10 hours needed for most casseroles.

Dried beans

Dried beans need soaking overnight in plenty of cold water before slow cooking. Alternatively, boil them in plenty of water for 2 minutes, allow them to soak (in the water in which

111

they were boiled) for 2 hours and then drain.

Because the cooking times vary so much (according to the type, size and age of the beans), at this stage I like to bring them to the boil in clean water for 10 minutes before draining and putting into the slow cooker. Red kidney beans should **always** be fast-boiled for 10 minutes before draining and transferring to the slow cooker – to destroy their toxins.

Lentils do not need soaking before cooking – just put them straight into the slow cooker.

Season dried beans after cooking, as salt tends to toughen the skins.

Ratatouille Niçoise

Serve hot or cold, as a starter course with crusty bread or as an accompaniment to meat or fish.

Serves 4-6   *LOW 5-7 hours*

4 tbsp olive oil
1 large onion, finely chopped
1 red pepper, seeds removed, diced
1 yellow pepper, seeds removed, diced
2 aubergines, diced
8 plum tomatoes, peeled and roughly chopped
4 courgettes, cut into 5mm (¼ in) slices
2 garlic cloves, crushed
salt and freshly milled black pepper
2 tbsp chopped fresh basil
1 tbsp chopped fresh parsley
Parmesan cheese shavings, to serve (optional)

1. Heat the oil in a large saucepan, add the onion and red and yellow peppers and cook, stirring occasionally, until softened but not browned.

2. Add the aubergines, tomatoes, courgettes, garlic and seasoning and cook for a further few minutes, stirring occasionally. Transfer to the slow cooker.

3. Put the lid on and cook on LOW for 5-7 hours.

4. Adjust the seasoning to taste and, just before serving, stir in the basil and parsley. If wished, serve sprinkled with shavings of Parmesan cheese.

Tuna-filled Peppers

Choose peppers which are equal in size and which will stand upright during cooking. Serve as a starter or a supper dish. If wished, serve with a tomato sauce.

Serves 4   *LOW 4-6 hours*

4 medium red or yellow peppers
1 tbsp olive oil
1 medium onion, finely chopped
115g (4 oz) mushrooms, finely chopped
200g can tuna, drained and flaked
55g (2 oz) long grain rice, cooked
salt and freshly milled pepper
½ tsp dried oregano or thyme

1. Cut a shallow lid from the top of each pepper and discard. Remove the core and seeds, taking care not to cut through the wall of the pepper.

2. Heat the oil in a small pan, add the onion and cook, stirring occasionally, until softened but not browned.

3. Add the mushrooms and cook for a further minute.

4. Remove from the heat and stir in the tuna, rice, seasoning and herbs.

5. Spoon the mixture into the peppers and stand them upright in the slow cooker.

6. Put the lid on and cook on LOW for 4-6 hours.

Tomatoes Stuffed with Bacon and Mushrooms

Double the quantity to serve as a lunch or supper dish with warm wholemeal or granary bread.

Serves 4 as a starter   *LOW 2-3 hours*

4 medium tomatoes
1 tbsp olive oil
55g (2 oz) lean bacon, finely chopped
55g (2 oz) mushrooms, finely chopped
1 garlic clove, crushed
25g (1 oz) fresh white breadcrumbs
salt and freshly milled black pepper
good pinch of dried thyme or mint

1. Slice the top off each tomato and, with a small spoon, carefully scoop out the pulp.

2. Heat the oil in a small pan, add the bacon and cook, stirring occasionally, until golden brown and cooked through.

3. Stir in the mushrooms and garlic and cook for a minute over a low heat.

4. Remove from the heat and stir in the breadcrumbs, seasoning and herbs.

5. Spoon the mixture into the tomatoes and stand them in the slow cooker.

6. Put the lid on and cook on LOW for 2-3 hours.

Stuffed Marrow

Choose the shape and size of your marrow to suit the shape and size of your slow cooker. Trim and halve the marrow lengthways, scoop out the seeds and lay it on its side, or slice it thickly, remove the seeds and stand the rings side by side.

Serves 4   *LOW 6-9 hours*

1 marrow
salt and freshly milled black pepper
1 tbsp oil
450g (1 lb) lean minced beef
1 medium onion, finely chopped
25g (1 oz) fresh breadcrumbs
1 roasted red pepper (from a jar or can), finely chopped
½ tsp Tabasco sauce
1 tbsp Worcestershire sauce
1 tsp paprika pepper
1 tbsp tomato purée

1. Peel and trim the marrow and either cut in half length-ways or cut through the middle (see note above). Using a knife and spoon, scoop out the seeds and discard. Sprinkle the inside of the marrow lightly with salt and pepper.

2. Heat the oil in a non-stick frying pan, add the beef and cook, stirring occasionally, until lightly browned. Add the onion and cook for a further minute.

3. Put the remaining ingredients into a bowl, add the beef and onion, season and mix well.

4. Spoon the mixture into the hollows of the marrow.

5. If the marrow is to stand on end, wrap each piece securely in foil and stand side by side in the slow cooker. If it is to lie on its side, sandwich the two halves together before wrapping securely in foil.

6. Put into the slow cooker and pour in sufficient boiling water to come half way up the marrow.

7. Put the lid on and cook on LOW for 6-9 hours.

Savoury Rice with Rosemary

The rosemary imparts a delicate fragrance to the rice.

Serves 4   *LOW 2-3 hours*

15g (½ oz) butter
2 tsp olive oil
2 lean streaky bacon rashers, finely chopped
1 medium onion, finely chopped
2 celery sticks, thinly sliced
1 small red pepper, seeds removed and diced
1 garlic clove, crushed
175g (6 oz) easy-cook long grain rice
600ml (1 pint) chicken stock
1 tsp chopped fresh rosemary leaves or ½ tsp dried
**   rosemary**
salt and freshly milled black pepper

1. Heat the butter and oil in a saucepan, add the bacon and cook, stirring occasionally, until lightly browned.

2. Add the onion, celery, red pepper and garlic and cook, stirring occasionally, until softened but not browned.

3. Stir in the rice and cook for 2 minutes.

4. Add the remaining ingredients and bring to the boil. Stir well and transfer to the slow cooker.

5. Put the lid on and cook on LOW for 2-3 hours, stirring once or twice during the final hour if possible.

Gabriel Potatoes

This dish is named in honour of Madame Gabriel who lived near Lyons. It is my slow-cook version of the wonderful gratin dauphinoise that she cooked for us each time we visited, even in the height of summer.

Serves 4   *LOW 7-9 hours*

1 tbsp olive oil, plus extra for greasing
115g (4 oz) lean bacon, chopped
1 medium onion, finely chopped
115g (4 oz) grated cheese such as mozzarella, Gruyère
  or Cheddar
1kg (2 lb 4 oz) potatoes, peeled and thinly sliced
1 tbsp dried herbs, such as oregano or thyme
salt and freshly milled black pepper
425ml (¾ pint) milk
2 medium eggs, beaten

1. Lightly grease the inside of the slow cooker and preheat on HIGH.

2. Heat the oil in a frying pan, add the bacon and cook, stirring occasionally, until crisp and golden brown. Using a slotted spoon, lift out and mix with the onion and cheese.

3. Put a layer of potatoes into the base of the slow cooker and sprinkle with the herbs and seasoning. Cover with a layer of the cheese mixture. Repeat until all the ingredients are used up, finishing with a layer of cheese.

4. Heat the milk until hot but not boiling and pour over the eggs, mixing well. Strain the mixture over the potatoes.

5. Cover and cook on LOW for 7-9 hours.

Curried Vegetables

Good served with freshly cooked basmati rice and raita (thick plain yoghurt, diced cucumber and mint), or with poppadums and mango chutney.

Serves 4   *LOW 7-9 hours*

1 tbsp oil
1 medium onion, finely chopped
1 small head of celery, thinly sliced
1 red pepper, seeds removed, roughly chopped
115g (4 oz) red lentils
1 tbsp curry paste
1 tsp turmeric
1 tsp cumin
1 tsp dried chilli
300ml (½ pint) vegetable stock
2 tbsp mango chutney, large pieces finely chopped
400g can chopped tomatoes
1 tbsp lemon juice
2 tbsp tomato purée
salt

1.   Heat the oil in a large frying pan, add the onion, celery and red pepper and cook, stirring occasionally, until softened but not browned.

2.   Add the remaining ingredients and stir well. Bring to the boil and transfer to the slow cooker.

3.   Put the lid on and cook on LOW for 7-9 hours.

Root Vegetable and Lentil Casserole

Use your favourite winter vegetables. I serve this casserole in shallow bowls and accompanied with thickly sliced French bread that has been topped with cheese and grilled until bubbling.

Serves 4-6   *LOW 3-6 hours*

2 tbsp olive oil
1 medium onion, thinly sliced into rings
2 celery sticks, sliced
2 medium carrots, sliced
1 large parsnip, cut into cubes
2 sweet potatoes, cut into cubes
1 small celeriac, cut into cubes
1 fennel bulb, trimmed and sliced
2 garlic cloves, crushed
140g (5 oz) green lentils
200g can chopped tomatoes
600ml (1 pint) vegetable stock
1 tsp dried mixed herbs
salt and freshly milled black pepper
chopped fresh herbs, such as parsley, coriander or
   chives

1. Heat the oil in a large saucepan, add the onion, celery and carrots and cook, stirring occasionally, until softened but not browned.

2. Add the parsnip, sweet potatoes, celeriac, fennel and garlic and cook for a further few minutes, stirring occasionally.

3. Stir in the lentils, tomatoes, stock, herbs and seasoning, bring to the boil and transfer to the slow cooker.

4. Put the lid on and cook on LOW for 3-6 hours.

5. Stir gently, adjusting the seasoning to taste, and scatter fresh herbs over each serving.

Chilli Bean Salad

Serve hot or at room temperature in bowls with hot garlic bread.

Serves 4-6   *LOW 4-8 hours*

2 tbsp olive oil
1 large onion, thinly sliced
1 large carrot, finely diced
1 garlic clove, crushed
2 tbsp red wine vinegar
400g can chopped tomatoes
1 tsp sugar
2-3 tsp chilli sauce
6 thin slices of fresh lemon, each cut into quarters
400g haricot beans, drained
400g flageolet beans, drained
400g can red kidney beans, drained
salt and freshly milled black pepper
chopped fresh parsley
crumbled feta cheese, to serve (optional)

1.   Heat the oil in a large saucepan, add the onion and carrot and cook, stirring occasionally, until softened.

2.   Add the garlic and cook for a further few minutes, stirring occasionally, until very soft and lightly browned. Transfer to the slow cooker.

3.   Stir in the remaining ingredients, except the herbs and cheese.

4.   Put the lid on and cook on LOW for 4-8 hours.

5.   Adjust the seasoning and serve sprinkled with parsley and (if using) crumbled cheese.

7

PUDDINGS

I still find it surprising that slow cookers excel when it comes to puddings. When you steam sponge or suet puddings in a slow cooker, the stodgy desserts of your schooldays will become just a memory. Slow cooking produces puddings that are light and moist. Furthermore, the kitchen won't be filled with steam for hours at a time.

Cooking fruit on the hob normally requires careful attention – turn your back on the saucepan for a minute and poached apple becomes apple purée in a trice. In a slow cooker, fruit retains its shape and texture so it can be used in flans, pies or as a refreshing chilled dessert.

Guidelines for Steamed Puddings

1. Preheat the slow cooker on HIGH.

2. Use a basin or soufflé dish that fits easily into the slow cooker. Cover it securely with greased greaseproof paper, baking paper or foil, leaving room for the pudding to rise.

3. Use the lifting strap described on page 25 to lower the basin into the slow cooker.

4. Pour round sufficient boiling water to come half way up the bowl or dish.

5. Put the lid on. Puddings containing a raising agent must be cooked on HIGH throughout to ensure a good rise. Do not exceed the 3-4 hours' cooking time recommended, otherwise the pudding may become dry.

Guidelines for Poached Fruit

1. Switch on the slow cooker, add 600ml (1 pint) boiling water and stir in the sugar until dissolved. The quantity of sugar depends on taste and the natural sweetness of the fruit.

2. Prepare the fruit as normal and slice or leave whole.

3. Put the fruit in the syrup, making sure that fruit that is likely to discolour (such as apple) is immersed during cooking.

4. Put the lid on and cook on LOW or HIGH. Cooking times will vary according to the size and ripeness of the fruit.

GUIDE TO COOKING TIMES FOR FRUIT	
Apples, pears (whole)	LOW 5-10 hours
Apples, pears (sliced)	LOW 2-5 hours
Berry fruits	LOW 2-4 hours

5. If your slow cooker has a removable pot, you can cover the cooked fruit with crumble, pastry or meringue and then finish cooking in the oven.

Honeyed Pears

Use honey with a good flavour for best results. A vegetable peeler will quickly and easily remove strips of rind from the lemon. Serve chilled with Greek yoghurt.

Serves 4   *LOW 5-10 hours*

4 medium pears, peeled, halved and cored
1 tbsp lemon juice
25g (1 oz) toasted hazelnuts, chopped
4 tbsp clear honey
425ml (¾ pint) apple juice, grape juice or water
pared rind of 1 lemon

1. Place the pears, cut side down, in the slow cooker. Sprinkle with the lemon juice and hazelnuts.

2. In a small pan (or in the microwave), heat the honey and apple juice gently with the lemon rind, stirring until the honey has dissolved. Pour over the pears.

3. Put the lid on and cook on LOW for 5-10 hours, spooning the juices over the pears towards the end of cooking if possible.

4. Remove the lemon rind and transfer to a serving dish to cool. Chill until required.

Mixed Fruit Compote

Serve chilled for breakfast or as a dessert with Greek yoghurt, thick cream or custard.

Serves 4   *LOW 6-10 hours*

225g (8 oz) mixed dried fruit, such as apples, prunes, pears, apricots and peaches (not the ready-to-eat varieties)
25g (1 oz) sultanas
25g (1 oz) raisins
2 tbsp toasted flaked almonds
2 tbsp caster sugar
600ml (1 pint) apple juice, orange juice or water
2 tbsp orange liqueur

1. Place all the ingredients, except the liqueur, in the slow cooker and stir well.

2. Put the lid on and cook on LOW for 6-10 hours.

3. Transfer to a serving dish and leave to cool before adding the orange liqueur.

Fragrant Rhubarb Meringue

You will need a slow cooker with a removable pot for this recipe. Otherwise, cook the rhubarb base in the slow cooker then transfer to an ovenproof dish before adding the meringue topping. Serve warm or chilled. (Of course, you can always cook the rhubarb as below and serve it chilled with whipped cream and crisp biscuits.)

Serves 4   *LOW 2½-3½ hours*

675g (1½ lb) fresh rhubarb, cut into 2.5cm (1 in) lengths
85g (3 oz) sugar
300ml (½ pint) unsweetened orange juice or water
3 fresh mint leaves, chopped

Meringue
2 medium egg whites
85g (3 oz) caster sugar

1.   Put the rhubarb into the slow cooker.

2.   Put the sugar, orange juice and mint into a small saucepan. Bring slowly to the boil, stirring, until the sugar has just dissolved. Remove from the heat, cover and leave to stand (to infuse) for 10 minutes.

3.   Strain the liquid and pour over the rhubarb.

4.   Put the lid on and cook on LOW for 2½-3½ hours.

5.   Preheat the oven to 200°C (400°F), gas 6. Whisk the egg whites until they stand in peaks. Add the sugar and whisk until stiff. If the rhubarb has produced a lot of juice, spoon out the extra liquid before spreading the meringue over the fruit. Bake in the hot oven for 10-15 minutes until golden brown.

Spiced Rhubarb

Follow the recipe for Fragrant Rhubarb replacing the mint with ½ tsp mixed spice and 2 tbsp marmalade. There is no need to strain the hot syrup before adding it to the slow cooker.

Baked Apples with Fruit and Nuts

Vary the filling if you like – try chopped dried apricots or dates in place of sultanas, chopped pistachios instead of hazelnuts or mixed spice instead of cinnamon. Serve warm with single cream, Greek yoghurt or custard.

Serves 4   *LOW 2-4 hours*

4 medium cooking apples, such as Bramley
25g (1 oz) sultanas
55g (2 oz) brown sugar
2 tbsp chopped toasted hazelnuts
¼ tsp ground cinnamon

1. Core the apples and, using a sharp knife, score a line around the 'equator' of each apple (but do not cut right through).

2. Mix together the sultanas, sugar, hazelnuts and cinnamon and spoon this mixture into the apples.

3. Stand the apples in the slow cooker and add 4 tbsp cold water.

4. Put the lid on and cook on LOW for 2-4 hours.

Tipsy Apricots

Serve chilled with whipped cream or a good-quality vanilla ice cream and crisp sweet biscuits. Instead of gin, you could use brandy or apricot liqueur.

Serves 4   *LOW 2-3 hours*

55g (2 oz) caster sugar
450g (1 lb) fresh apricots
vanilla extract
2 tbsp gin

1. Put 150ml (¼ pint) boiling water and the sugar into the slow cooker and switch to HIGH.

2. Meanwhile, using a sharp knife, cut each apricot in half and remove the stone.

3. Stir the sugar until it has dissolved and add the apricots, cut side down. Add a few drops of vanilla extract.

4. Put the lid on and cook on LOW for 2-3 hours.

5. Transfer to a serving dish, stir in the gin and leave to cool. Chill until required.

Apple Dumplings

A filling pudding that is a real winter treat. Use beef or vegetable suet as you prefer. Serve with custard or pouring cream.

Serves 4   *HIGH 3-4 hours*

Suet crust
225g (8 oz) self-raising flour
115g (4 oz) shredded suet
pinch of ground cloves or mixed spice

butter for greasing
4 medium cooking apples, such as Bramleys, peeled and cored
4 tbsp mincemeat

1.   Preheat the slow cooker on HIGH.

2.   Meanwhile, make the suet pastry by mixing together the flour, suet and spice, adding sufficient water to make a soft dough. Cut the pastry into four equal pieces and, on a lightly floured surface, roll out each one into a circle large enough to enclose an apple.

3.   Cut four squares of foil slightly larger than the pastry and grease with butter. Stand an apple on each pastry circle and fill with the mincemeat. Moisten the edges of the pastry with water and fold over the apple, crimping the edges until well sealed. Stand a dumpling in each foil square and fold to form a loose, well sealed parcel.

4.   Stand the parcels in the slow cooker and add boiling water to 2.5cm (1 in) depth.

5.   Put the lid on and cook on HIGH for 3-4 hours.

Creamy Rice Pudding

If possible, it's a good idea to stir the pudding once or twice during the final stages of cooking.

Serves 4   *LOW 6-8 hours*

Butter for greasing
55g (2 oz) pudding rice, rinsed
55g (2 oz) sugar
600ml (1 pint) milk
150ml (¼ pint) double cream
good pinch of grated nutmeg

1.   Butter the inside of the slow cooker.

2.   Put the rice and sugar into the pot and stir well. Mix the milk with the cream and pour over. Sprinkle with nutmeg.

3.   Put the lid on and cook on LOW for 6-8 hours.

Crème Caramel

To make Egg Custard, omit the caramel, sprinkle the surface with grated nutmeg before cooking and do not turn the pudding out of its dish.

Serves 4   *LOW 3-4 hours*

butter for greasing

Caramel
4 tbsp granulated sugar
4 tbsp water

Custard
425ml (¾ pint) milk
3 medium eggs
½ tsp vanilla extract
55g (2 oz) caster sugar

1.   Butter a 600ml (1 pint) soufflé dish.

2.   Make the caramel. Put the granulated sugar and water into a saucepan on medium heat and bring to the boil without stirring. Continue bubbling until the syrup turns golden brown and remove from the heat immediately.

3.   Pour the caramel into the dish and swirl around to coat the base.

4.   In a small saucepan, heat the milk until hot but not boiling.

5.   Beat the eggs with vanilla extract and caster sugar and stir in the hot milk. Strain over the caramel in the dish. Cover with foil and, using the lifting strap (see page 25), lower into the slow cooker. Pour round sufficient boiling water to come half way up the sides of the dish.

6.   Put the lid on and cook on LOW for 3-4 hours.

7.   Carefully lift the dish out and leave to cool. Chill for several hours before turning out on to a serving dish.

Cappuccino Cream

Serve with ratafias or other crisp biscuits.

Serves 4   *LOW 3-4 hours*

butter for greasing
600ml (1 pint) milk
55g (2 oz) caster sugar
1 tbsp instant coffee granules
4 medium eggs
whipped cream
grated chocolate

1.   Butter a 1 litre (1¾ pint) soufflé dish.

2.   Heat the milk in a saucepan until hot but not boiling.
     Add the sugar and coffee and stir until dissolved. Beat
     the eggs and stir in the hot milk. Strain the mixture into
     the dish.

3.   Cover with foil and, using the lifting strap (see page 25),
     lower into the slow cooker. Pour round sufficient boiling
     water to come half way up the sides of the dish.

4.   Put the lid on and cook on LOW for 3-4 hours.

5.   Carefully lift the dish out and leave to cool. Chill until
     required. To serve, top with whipped cream and grated
     chocolate.

Golden Suet Pudding

This is one of those old-fashioned puddings that wouldn't be complete without hot custard.

Serves 4   *HIGH 3-4 hours*

butter
115g (4 oz) self-raising flour
pinch of salt
55g (2 oz) shredded suet
55g (2 oz) caster sugar
1 medium egg, beaten
2 tbsp milk
3 tbsp golden syrup

1. Preheat the slow cooker on HIGH. Butter a 600ml (1 pint) pudding basin.

2. Mix the flour and salt and stir in the suet and sugar. Add the egg and milk and mix to a firm consistency.

3. Spoon the golden syrup into the pudding basin and top with the pudding mixture.

4. Cover securely with greased greaseproof paper or foil. Using the lifting strap (see page 25), lower the basin into the slow cooker. Pour round sufficient boiling water to come half way up the sides of the basin.

5. Put the lid on and cook on HIGH for 3-4 hours.

6. Carefully lift the basin out of the slow cooker and turn the pudding out on to a warmed serving dish.

Date and Walnut Pudding

Serve it with butterscotch sauce and a spoonful of thick yoghurt.

Serves 4   *HIGH 3-4 hours*

55g (2 oz) butter, softened, plus extra for greasing
55g (2 oz) caster sugar
1 medium egg, beaten
85g (3 oz) self-raising flour
25g (1 oz) stoned dates, finely chopped
25g (1 oz) walnuts, chopped
1 tbsp milk

1. Preheat the slow cooker on HIGH. Butter a 600ml (1 pint) pudding basin.

2. Beat the butter with the sugar until pale and fluffy. Beat in the egg and fold in half the flour and all the dates and walnuts. Fold in the remaining flour and the milk.

3. Spoon the mixture into the basin.

4. Cover securely with greased greaseproof paper or foil. Using the lifting strap (see page 25), lower the basin into the slow cooker. Pour round sufficient boiling water to come half way up the sides of the basin.

5. Put the lid on and cook on HIGH for 3-4 hours.

6. Carefully lift the basin out of the slow cooker and turn the pudding out on to a warmed serving dish.

Orange and Sultana Roll

A variation on the nursery pudding called jam roly poly. Serve it with plenty of thick oustard.

Serves 4-6   *HIGH 3-4 hours*

225g (8 oz) self-raising flour
115g (4 oz) shredded suet
8 tbsp orange marmalade
55g (2 oz) sultanas
½ tsp ground cinnamon
butter

1. Preheat the slow cooker on HIGH.

2. Meanwhile, make the suet pastry by mixing together the flour and suet, adding sufficient water to make a soft dough.

3. On a lightly floured surface, roll out the pastry to a rectangle 5mm (¼ in) thick and no wider than the diameter of your slow cooker. Moisten the edges with water. Spread the marmalade over the pastry, leaving the edges clear. Sprinkle with sultanas and cinnamon. Roll up the pastry from a short end and pinch together the dampened edges.

4. Butter a large square of foil, place the roll on it and wrap loosely. Seal the ends securely. Place in the slow cooker with the seam uppermost. Pour around sufficient boiling water to come half way up the parcel.

5. Put the lid on and cook on HIGH for 3-4 hours.

Apple and Banana Pudding

Serves 4-5   *HIGH 3-4 hours*

Butter for greasing

Suet crust
225g (8 oz) self-raising flour
115g (4 oz) shredded suet
pinch of ground cinnamon (optional)

Filling
115g (4 oz) soft brown sugar
¼ tsp ground cinnamon
675g (1½ lb) cooking apples, such as Bramley, peeled, cored and sliced
3 bananas, peeled and sliced

1. Preheat the slow cooker on HIGH. Butter a 1 litre (1¾ pint) pudding basin.

2. Mix together the flour, suet, cinnamon (if using) and sufficient water to make a soft dough. Reserve one-third for the lid and roll out the remainder on a lightly floured surface and use to line the pudding basin.

3. Mix the brown sugar with the cinnamon. Pack the lined basin firmly with layers of apple, sprinkled with the sugar mixture, and banana. (The pudding should not quite fill the basin – to allow space for the crust to rise.)

4. Roll out the remaining pastry to form the lid. Moisten the edges of the pudding with water and press the lid into position.

5. Cover with greased greaseproof paper or foil and lower into the slow cooker using a lifting strap (see page 25). Pour in sufficient boiling water to come half way up the side of the basin.

6. Put the lid on and cook on HIGH for 3-4 hours.

Golden Lemon Pudding

Sometimes I use orange rind and juice in place of lemon, and maple syrup in place of golden syrup.

Serves 4-6   *HIGH 3-4 hours*

115g (4 oz) butter, softened, plus extra for greasing
55g (2 oz) caster sugar
2 tbsp golden syrup
55g (2 oz) chopped mixed nuts
2 tbsp lemon juice
finely grated rind of 1 lemon
2 medium eggs, lightly beaten
225g (8 oz) self-raising flour

1. Preheat the slow cooker on HIGH. Butter a 1 litre (1¾ pint) pudding basin.

2. Put all the ingredients into a large bowl and beat until well mixed. Spoon the mixture into the basin.

3. Cover with greased greaseproof paper or foil and lower into the slow cooker using a lifting strap (see page 25). Pour in sufficient boiling water to come half way up the side of the basin.

4. Put the lid on and cook on HIGH for 3-4 hours.

Christmas Pudding

The slow cooker makes cooking the Christmas pudding a convenient affair. And it is a great advantage to be able to reheat the pudding in the slow cooker on Christmas morning, when the hob is usually full. This pudding was originally developed by Sheila, a home economist who inspired me greatly. It has been enjoyed by my family for many years.

Makes two 1 litre (1¾ pint) puddings   *HIGH 10-12 hours*

oil for greasing
175g (6 oz) beef or vegetable suet
175g (6 oz) fresh breadcrumbs
115g (4 oz) plain flour
good pinch of salt
½ tsp ground cinnamon
½ tsp ground mace
½ tsp ground nutmeg
¼ tsp ground ginger
115g (4 oz) molasses sugar
115g (4 oz) light muscovado sugar
225g (8 oz) seedless raisins
225g (8 oz) sultanas
225g (8 oz) currants
1 medium cooking apple, peeled, cored and chopped
175g (6 oz) grated carrot
55g (2 oz) blanched almonds, roughly chopped
finely grated rind and juice of 1 medium orange
finely grated rind of 1 small lemon
3 large eggs, lightly beaten
2 tbsp brandy (optional)

1.   Grease two 1 litre (1¾ pint) pudding basins.

2.   In a large bowl, mix the suet with the breadcrumbs and add the flour, salt and spices. Stir in the sugars, add the dried fruit, apple, carrot and almonds and mix well.

3.   In a small bowl, mix the orange rind and juice with the lemon rind, eggs and brandy (if using). Stir into the dry ingredients until well mixed.

4.   Divide the mixture between the basins, levelling the tops with the back of a spoon. Cover with a double

thickness of oiled greaseproof paper, then cover with foil and secure with string. Alternatively, use heatproof plastic pudding basins with clip-on lids.

5. Allow one pudding to stand in a cool place for several hours or overnight. Refrigerate the other pudding.

6. Next day, preheat the slow cooker on HIGH for 30 minutes.

7. Using the lifting strap (see page 25), lower the pudding that wasn't refrigerated into the slow cooker and pour sufficient boiling water into the cooker to come within 2.5cm (1 in) of the top of the basin.

8. Put the lid on and cook on HIGH for 10-12 hours.

9. Remove the second pudding from the refrigerator, allow it to reach room temperature and cook as above.

10. After cooking, leave to cool. Wrap in extra foil and store in a cool dark place.

11. To reheat one pudding, remove the extra foil and put into the slow cooker. Add sufficient boiling water to come half way up the side of the basin. Put the lid on and cook on HIGH for 4 hours or on LOW overnight.

Bread and Butter Pudding

The pudding is a particular favourite with men. It's good made with sweet bread such as brioche too. Serve warm with cream for pouring.

Serves 4   *HIGH 3-5 hours*

5-6 thin slices of bread and butter, crusts removed
butter for greasing
25g (1 oz) currants
25g (1 oz) sultanas
25g (1 oz) dried apricots, chopped
15g (½ oz) chopped toasted nuts
2 medium eggs, lightly beaten
55g (2 oz) caster sugar
300ml (½ pint) milk

1.   Cut the bread and butter into small squares. Butter a 600ml (1 pint) soufflé dish.

2.   Place a layer of bread on the bottom of the dish and sprinkle with the currants. Cover with a second layer of bread and sprinkle with the sultanas. Cover with the final layer of bread and sprinkle with the apricots and nuts.

3.   Beat the eggs with the sugar. Heat the milk until hot but not boiling and pour over the egg mixture, stirring well to dissolve the sugar. Strain over the bread and, using the back of a spoon, gently press the bread down until it is immersed. Cover with buttered foil. Using the lifting strap (see page 25), lower the dish into the slow cooker and add sufficient boiling water to come half way up the dish.

4.   Put the lid on and cook on HIGH for 3-5 hours.

5.   Optional: before serving, brown the top of the pudding lightly under the grill.

8

ASSORTED EXTRAS

The more you use your slow cooker, the more things you will want to cook in it.

- Pâté can be cooked in a covered dish with sufficient boiling water poured round to come half way up its sides. Always cook on HIGH.

- Lemon curd cooks gently, without separating and with no need for stirring.

- Cheese fondue and hot dips can be heated and served in the slow cooker.

- Fruit for jams and marmalades can be left to soften in the slow cooker before transferring to a pan and fast boiling.

- Punch and mulled wine can be heated up in, and served straight from, the slow cooker.

- Bread flavoured with herb or garlic butter can be heated and kept warm in the slow cooker.

- Cakes and teabreads can be cooked in a cake tin. Although the result will not be as crisp or brown as oven-baked cakes, a thin coating of icing or a jam glaze can easily disguise it. In fact, chocolate cakes look attractive even without icing. Always cover the tin securely with foil, allowing room for the cake to rise. Pour round sufficient boiling water to come half way up its sides and put the lid on. Never try to cook them without adding water and always cook on HIGH.

- Check with your manufacturer's recipe book for other good ideas – like cooking porridge overnight or making chutney or relish.

Country Pâté

For the best texture, use a mincer to prepare this recipe – if you use a food processor, the result will be very smooth. Serve the pâté as a starter or light lunch with crisp biscuits or fresh crusty bread and salad garnish.

Serves 6   *HIGH 3-4 hours*

4 streaky bacon rashers, rinds removed
25g (1 oz) butter
1 medium onion, finely chopped
225g (8 oz) chicken livers
225g (8 oz) lamb's liver, cut into pieces
225g (8 oz) belly of pork, minced or very finely chopped
1 tsp salt
freshly milled black pepper
1 large garlic clove, crushed
½ tsp dried rosemary
1 medium egg, beaten
2 tbsp double cream

1. Preheat the slow cooker on HIGH.

2. Grease a small loaf or cake tin (make sure it will fit into the slow cooker) and line it with the bacon.

3. Heat the butter in a large frying pan, add the onion and cook, stirring occasionally, until softened but not browned. Add both types of liver and cook for 1 minute until stiffened. Remove from the heat and put this mixture through a mincer.

4. Combine the liver mixture with the remaining ingredients, mixing well, and pour into the prepared tin. Cover tightly with greased foil.

5. Lower the tin into the slow cooker using the lifting strap (see page 25) and add sufficient boiling water to come half way up its sides.

6. Put the lid on and cook on HIGH for 3-4 hours.

7. Lift out of the slow cooker, place a weight on top to compress it and leave to cool completely before turning out on to a serving plate.

Pâté Maison

You won't require a mincer or processor to make this pâté. A sharp knife is all you need.

Serves 6   *HIGH 3-4 hours*

25g (1 oz) butter
225g (8 oz) chicken livers
225g (8 oz) pork sausage meat
115g (4 oz) mushrooms, chopped
8 green olives stuffed with pimento, quartered, plus
   extra slices for garnish
1 large garlic clove, crushed
½ tsp dried mixed herbs
½ tsp salt
freshly milled black pepper

1. Preheat the slow cooker on HIGH.

2. Heat the butter in a frying pan, add the livers and cook quickly until browned on all sides. Remove from the heat and allow to cool while you prepare the remaining ingredients.

3. In a bowl, mix the sausage meat, mushrooms, olive quarters, garlic, herbs and seasoning.

4. Coarsely chop the livers and add to the mixture with the juices from the pan. Mix well and spoon into a 600ml (1 pint) soufflé dish. Cover tightly with greased foil.

5. Lower the dish into the slow cooker using the lifting strap (see page 25) and add sufficient boiling water to come half way up its sides.

6. Put the lid on and cook on HIGH for 3-4 hours.

7. Lift out of the slow cooker, place a weight on top to compress it and leave to cool completely. Serve garnished with olive slices.

Lemon Curd

Homemade curd is delicious. This one is particularly 'lemony'. Try using other citrus fruits too, such as oranges or limes.

Makes about 1kg (2 lb)   *LOW 3-4 hours*

115g (4 oz) butter
juice and finely grated rind of 4 lemons
450g (1 lb) caster sugar
4 medium eggs, beaten

1. Melt the butter in a pan and add the lemon juice, lemon rind and sugar. Remove from the heat, stir until the sugar has dissolved and allow to cool.

2. Stir the eggs into the lemon mixture and pour into a 1.2 litre (2 pint) basin. Cover tightly with foil.

3. Use the lifting strap (see page 25) to lower the basin into the slow cooker and add sufficient boiling water to come half way up its sides.

4. Put the lid on and cook on LOW for 3-4 hours.

5. Stir the curd, pour into clean, warmed jars and cover. Store in the refrigerator and use within three weeks.

Swiss Cheese Fondue

The secret of a successful fondue is gentle, even cooking. If it is heated too quickly, or if a metal pan is used, the fondue will separate into a rubbery mass with cheese-flavoured wine floating on top. In Switzerland an earthenware dish is used to cook a cheese fondue so the stoneware pot of a slow cooker is an excellent substitute.

Traditionally, this dish is prepared by the man of the house!

Use day-old French bread, cut into 25mm (1 in) cubes and make sure that each cube has a piece of crust attached. If the bread is too fresh it will become soggy and fall into the fondue.

Kirsch is normally the spirit used but is more expensive than vodka – I admit, I can hardly tell the difference.

Sometimes, I stir about 55g (2 oz) chopped, crisp-fried bacon into the fondue just before serving.

Serves 4   *LOW 1-3 hours*

1 clove garlic, halved
300ml (½ pint) dry white wine
1 tsp lemon juice
280g (10 oz) Emmenthal cheese, grated
280g (10 oz) Gruyère or Gouda cheese, grated
1 tbsp cornflour
white pepper
pinch of grated nutmeg
pinch of paprika pepper
3 tbsp vodka
French bread cubes

1. Rub the cut sides of the garlic over the inside of the slow cooker. Add the wine and lemon juice and switch to LOW.

2. Mix the two types of cheese with the cornflour, pepper, nutmeg and paprika and stir into the wine.

3. Put the lid on and heat on LOW for 1-3 hours, stirring occasionally.

4. Stir in the vodka just before serving. Serve the fondue, still in the slow cooker (disconnect it first), with bread for dipping.

Chocolate Fondue

Chocoholic? You'll love this!

Serves 4   *LOW 1-2½ hours*

200g (7 oz) plain chocolate
150ml (5 fl oz) double cream
¼ tsp ground cinnamon
¼ tsp grated nutmeg
3 tbsp orange liqueur, brandy or rum
25g (1 oz) toasted chopped mixed nuts
sponge finger cubes
selection of fresh fruit pieces, such as apple, pear,
**   oranges, pineapple**

1.   Preheat the slow cooker on HIGH.

2.   Break the chocolate into the slow cooker and add the
      cream, cinnamon and nutmeg.

3.   Heat on LOW for 1-2½ hours, stirring occasionally.

4.   Stir in the liqueur and chopped nuts just before serving.
      Serve the fondue, still in the slow cooker (disconnect it
      first), wlth sponge finger cubes and fruit for dipping.

Mulled Wine

Use an inexpensive red wine, adjusting the quantities of this warming tipple to suit the size of your slow cooker.

Serves 12 generous glasses   *HIGH 1 hour, plus*
LOW as long as it takes to drink

2 bottles of dry red wine
2 lemons
1 orange
4 whole cloves
pinch of ground cinnamon
115g (4 oz) sugar
2 tbsp orange liqueur or brandy

1.   Preheat the slow cooker on HIGH.

2.   Pour the wine into the slow cooker. Cut thin slivers of rind from one lemon (a vegetable peeler is ideal for the job) and squeeze the juice. Add the rind and juice to the slow cooker.

3.   Cut the orange in half. Stud one half with the cloves and float in the wine. Add the cinnamon.

4.   Heat on HIGH for 1 hour.

5.   Add the sugar, stirring until dissolved, then switch the slow cooker to LOW until required.

6.   To serve, remove the lemon rind and orange half. Stir in the orange liqueur or brandy. Thinly slice the remaining lemon and half orange and float on top of the mulled wine. Ladle straight from the slow cooker into suitable serving glasses.

Halloween Punch

The slow cooker heats the punch without boiling it.

Serves 9 generous glasses   *HIGH 1 hour, plus*
LOW as long as it takes to drink

1 litre (1¾ pints) dry cider
pinch of ground cinnamon
4 whole cloves
2 eating apples
2 tbsp muscovado sugar
1 orange
150ml (¼ pint) gin

1. Preheat the slow cooker on HIGH.

2. Pour the cider into the slow cooker and add the cinnamon. Stick the cloves into one apple and add it to the cider.

3. Heat on HIGH for 1 hour.

4. Remove the cloves from the apple and add the sugar, stirring until dissolved. Switch the slow cooker to LOW. Core the second apple (leave the skin on), cut into thin slices and add to the punch. Thinly slice the orange and add them too.

5. Stir in the gin just before serving. Ladle straight from the slow cooker into suitable serving glasses.

Herb and Garlic Bread

Hot bread flavoured with herbs and garlic – ready when you are.

Serves 4   *HIGH 1-2 hours*

Small brown loaf
55g (2 oz) butter, softened
1 tsp dried mixed herbs or 1-2 tbsp chopped fresh
   herbs such as parsley, chives or mint
1 garlic clove, crushed

1. Using a sharp knife, cut the bread into slices 1.5cm (½ in) thick, taking care not to cut through the bottom crust.

2. Mix the butter with the herbs and garlic.

3. Carefully spread the cut sides of the bread with the butter mixture. Shape a cap of foil over the bread to ensure that the slices do not fall apart during heating (don't wrap completely in foil otherwise the bread may become soggy).

4. Stand the bread in the slow cooker, put the lid on and heat on HIGH for 1-2 hours.

Banana Teabread

Serve sliced and spread with butter.

Serves 6-8   *HIGH 2-3 hours*

butter for greasing
175g (6 oz) self-raising flour
pinch of salt
¼ tsp ground cinnamon
85g (3 oz) butter
115g (4 oz) caster sugar
55g (2 oz) sultanas
55g (2 oz) walnuts, chopped
2 large, very ripe bananas
2 medium eggs, lightly beaten

1. Preheat the slow cooker on HIGH. Butter an 18cm (7 in) cake tin and line with baking paper.

2. Sift the flour with the salt and cinnamon. Rub in the butter until the mixture resembles fine breadcrumbs. Stir in the sugar, sultanas and walnuts.

3. Peel and mash the bananas. Beat the eggs into the banana and mix into the dry ingredients.

4. Spoon the mixture into the cake tin, level the top and cover securely with foil. Using the lifting strap (see page 25), lower the tin into the slow cooker and add sufficient boiling water to come half way up its sides.

5. Cook on HIGH for 2-3 hours. If wished, remove the foil and brown the top of the cake under a hot grill. Turn out on to a wire rack and allow to cool.

Chocolate Cake

Chocolate cake is a favourite of most people. Here's how to make it in the slow cooker.

Serves 6   *HIGH 3-4 hours*

butter for greasing
1 tbsp cocoa powder
115g (4 oz) butter, softened
115g (4 oz) caster sugar
2 medium eggs
115g (4 oz) self-raising flour, sieved

Icing
2 tbsp cocoa powder
85g (3 oz) butter, softened
225g (8 oz) icing sugar
2 tbsp milk
grated chocolate to decorate (optional)

1. Preheat the slow cooker on HIGH. Butter an 18cm (7 in) cake tin.

2. Blend the cocoa powder with 2 tbsp hot water and allow to cool.

3. Beat the butter and sugar until light and fluffy.

4. Beat in the cocoa mixture and the eggs, one at a time, adding a little of the sieved flour with the eggs. Using a metal tablespoon, gently fold in the remaining flour.

5. Spoon the mixture into the tin and smooth the top. Cover securely with foil. Using the lifting strap (see page 25), lower the tin into the slow cooker and add sufficient boiling water to come half way up its sides.

6. Put the lid on and cook on HIGH for 3-4 hours.

7. Turn out on to a wire rack and allow to cool completely.

8. To make the icing, blend the cocoa powder with 2 tbsp hot water and allow to cool. Beat the butter, adding the icing sugar, milk and cocoa mixture, until smooth and fairly soft.

9. Halve the cake horizontally and sandwich with half the butter icing. Spread the remaining icing over the top and decorate with grated chocolate if using.

Black Forest Cherry Gateau

Prepare the cake as opposite. Split into three layers and sandwich together with whipped cream and black cherry pie filling. Decorate the top and sides with whipped cream and grated plain chocolate.

INDEX

In the same series

EAT MEDITERRANEAN

Annette Yates's easy-to-follow recipes show how, by using a few simple good-quality ingredients, you can bring the sun-drenched flavours of the Mediterranean to your own table at any time of the year.

PRESSURE COOKING PROPERLY EXPLAINED

The ideal introduction to pressure cooking for newcomers and for those whose pressure cooker lies unused at the back of the cupboard. Dianne Page's book is packed with simple recipes for quick, tasty, nourishing meals.

THE FAN OVEN BOOK

Jenny Webb helps you to understand how your fan oven works, and how to get the best from it. She includes a simple-to-use conversion chart so you can easily convert the temperatures or settings you used in your former conventional oven to the new ones you'll need now. Her book is full of delicious recipes designed specifically for the fan oven.

Uniform with this book

In the same series

THE BLENDER BOOK

Get the most from your blender! Annette Yates gives easy-to-follow blender recipes for bastes, pastes and marinades; spreads, pâtés and dips; dressings, sauces and soups; sweet and savoury tarts; delightful desserts; shakes, smoothies and cocktails.

BIG ON FLAVOUR, LOW IN FAT

Caroline Young's recipes are quick to prepare. They're low in fat but simply bursting with flavour. Made with fresh, colourful ingredients, they look great on the plate, and are in very generous portions as well.

STEAMING!

Annette Yates offers here a larder-full of new recipes, combining healthy, low-fat meal ideas with traditional hearty fare. Cooking charts give steaming times for all kinds of food, in addition to the numerous recipes for eggs, vegetables, couscous, rice, pasta, fish, poultry, meat, desserts, parcels and wraps.

Uniform with this book

MICROWAVE COOKING PROPERLY EXPLAINED

Whether you are a new microwave owner or an experienced user, Annette Yates will help you get the most from your microwave. The recipes she includes cook successfully in a variety of microwave ovens and all have been tested and acclaimed by her family and friends.

MICROWAVE COOKING TIMES AT A GLANCE !

The essential guide for everyone with a microwave. Full of tips and hints about preparing and cooking different types of food, as well as the length of cooking time required, with tables giving at-a-glance advice for all wattages 500W to 1000W. Arranged in A-Z sequence for speedy reference.

THE COMBINATION MICROWAVE COOK

At last, a cookbook written specifically for combination microwave cookers and for microwaves with built-in grills. Contains over 100 recipes, all developed to make full use of these modern appliances. Every recipe is marked with symbols so that you can see immediately whether it is suitable for cooking on combination or microwave + grill, or both.

To order the following Right Way titles, please fill in the form below

No. of copies	Title	Price	Total
	Pressure Cooking Properly Explained	£4.99	
	Steaming!	£3.99	
	The Blender Book	£3.99	
	For P&P add £2.50 for the first book, £1 for each additional book		
	Grand Total		£

Name: _____

Address: _____

_____ Postcode: _____

Daytime Tel. No./Email _____
(in case of query)

Three ways to pay:
  1. Telephone the TBS order line on 01206 255 800.
     Order lines are open Monday – Friday, 8:30am – 5:30pm.

  2. I enclose a cheque made payable to **TBS Ltd** for £_____

  3. Please charge my [ ] Visa [ ] Mastercard [ ] Amex [ ] Maestro (issue no)

     Card number: _____

     Expiry date: _____ Last three digits on back of card: _____

     Signature: _____
                (your signature is essential when paying by credit or debit card)

Please return forms to Cash Sales/Direct Mail Dept., The Book Service, Colchester Road, Frating Green, Colchester CO7 7DW.

Enquiries to readers@constablerobinson.com.

Constable and Robinson Ltd (directly or via its agents) may mail, email or phone you about promotions or products.

[ ] Tick box if you do not want these from us [ ] or our subsidiaries.

www.right-way.co.uk
www.constablerobinson.com